I0521668

ANUNNAKI RITES

THE MAQLU RITUAL BOOK

NEW STANDARD ZUIST EDITION

POCKET EDITION

Published from
Mardukite Borsippa HQ, San Luis Valley, Colorado
Founding Church of Mardukite Zuism,
Mardukite Academy & Systemology Society
for religious and educational purposes only.

ANUNNAKI RITES

THE MAQLU RITUAL BOOK

NEW STANDARD ZUIST EDITION

Developed by Joshua Free for the
Church of Mardukite Zuism

THE JOSHUA FREE IMPRINT
JFI PUBLICATIONS

© 2022, JOSHUA FREE

ISBN : 979-8-9864379-3-4

A special pocket version of
The Maqlu Ritual Book
edited for founding the
Church of Mardukite Zuism

Pocket Paperback Edition — *July 2022*

Also available in hardcover as
"The Maqlu Ritual Book"

mardukite.com

The _Original_ Cuneiform Spellbook of Rites

Here are the ancient Sumerian Anunnaki rites
that inspired magical systems on Earth today.

Here is the cuneiform tablet series of the
ancient Mardukite Babylonian Maqlu Ritual,
fully translated and restored for a special
pocket paperback edition commemorating a
decade of its inclusion in
"The Complete Anunnaki Bible."

Here are the "original" Anunnaki Rites,
drawing from the oldest writings on the planet
—separating "prehistory" from "history"—
Babylonian cuneiform Mesopotamian sources.

Here is the recovery and incorporation of
wisdom from the Ancient Near East into
a modern tradition of Babylonian
Neopaganism known for over a decade as
Mardukite Zuism.

This edition combines "Mardukite Zuism:
A Brief Introduction" with all the original
"M-Series" and "Liber-M" records from
the Mardukite Research Organization.

Here is the New Standard Zuist Edition of the
classic text by world renowned Joshua Free;
a special pocket paperback version of
"The Maqlu Ritual Book"
edited for the Church of Mardukite Zuism.

MARDUKITE ZUISM

TABLET OF CONTENTS

THE ORIGINAL
MARDUKITE "LIBER-M" ARCHIVES

THE MAQLU RITUAL
CUNEIFORM TABLET SERIES

APPENDIX

PUBLISHER'S PREFACE TO THE
NEW STANDARD ZUIST EDITION

More than a decade since a newly translated edition of *"Liber-M"* material integrated with Joshua Free's *"Mardukite Core"* circulating underground, a pocket *"NSZE"* paperback edition is now available as an alternative to the collector's edition hardcover released in 2019 as *"The Maqlu Ritual Book."*

The *"NSZE"* series of *Anunnaki Bibles* and other devotional supplements simplify a new futurist presentation of original cuneiform tablet translations from *The Complete Anunnaki Legacy*—the result of over half-of-a-decade of intensive explorations by Mardukite Research Organization (Mardukite Chamberlains/Council of Nabu) from 2008-2015.

For the first time in modern history, all of humanity can access this collection of concise *cuneiform liturgical* translations—composing a profound ritual in itself: the *Maqlu*, an inspiration for magical protection, banishing rituals and exorcisms in religious and spiritual systems on planet Earth for thousands of years thereafter. *An original cuneiform classic!*

MARDUKITE

ZUISM

A BRIEF
INTRODUCTION

*According to the most ancient
historical records
written at the birth of our
modern civilization...* *

432,000 YEARS AGO...[*]

a small population of advanced beings—called the <u>ANUNNAKI</u>—began developing the planet Earth for their purposes. These elite Self-Actualized spiritual beings resided on Earth in physical bodies, but found their forms inadequate for the physical labors required. Enter: the "Human Condition." Ancient "<u>cuneiform</u>" tablet writings from Sumerians and Babylonians of Mesopotamia are clear regarding the original creation and systematic programming of Humanity.

CUNEIFORM...

is the oldest known writing system used by scribes of ancient Babylon to record their wisdom and the history of humanity on <u>clay tablets</u>. "Cuneiform" is named for its style of wedge-shaped script formed by a <u>reed pen</u> called a "<u>stylus.</u>" Rather than an alphabet of letters, cuneiform is a system of "<u>signs</u>" representing "things" and "ideas." These may be combined to represent even more complex "signs."

---

[*] First published in 2019 as *"Mardukite Zuism: A Brief Introduction."*

Many concepts adopted for modern "<u>Mardukite Zuism</u>" are derived from cuneiform tablets.The ANUNNAKI introduced complex writing systems in order to program civilization and all parameters of Reality for the Human Condition. Legendary "<u>Tablets of Destiny</u>" (Divine Truth, supreme knowledge and cosmic power of the "gods") were first introduced to Humanity in the Babylonian narrative known best as the "<u>Epic of Creation</u>".

THE ARCANE TABLETS.

Ancient Babylonians used the Tablets of Destiny & Creation Epic to systematize all cosmic knowledge into a workable <u>paradigm</u> called "Mardukite Zuism"—a <u>systemology</u> received directly from the ANUNNAKI.

<u>Paradigm</u> : an all-encompassing standard or religion used to view the world and communicate reality.

<u>Systemology</u> : applied philosophies of Mardukite Zuism combined with personal spiritual techniques and technology ("Tech") that is effectively demonstrating systematic principles of a "paradigm."

THE EPIC OF CREATION.

Seven cuneiform tablets compose the ancient Babylonian Epic of Creation, named the Enuma Eliš by scholars after its opening lines. These seven tablets are the basis for what later traditions refer to as the *"Seven Days of Creation."* The *Epic of Creation* tablets describe development of all existences with a Divine artistic perfection. The Enuma Eliš is the core example of religious literature from Babylon, which served as the basis for ancient *"Mardukite Zuism"*—the first true systematized religion in history.

THE SYSTEMOLOGY OF LIFE, UNIVERSES & EVERYTHING.

The *Arcane Tablets* describe the division of the ALL by the LAW, outside of which is but INFINITY. The *Epic of Creation* describes these activities as "mythology."

The Mardukite Systemology "Standard Model" uses the same information to demonstrates...

that <u>ALL</u> ("AN-KI") envelops both:
the <u>Spiritual Existences</u> ("AN")
and the <u>Physical Existences</u> ("KI")
divided by <u>Cosmic Law</u> and
connected by <u>Life-Awareness</u> ("ZU")
and beyond which is only the <u>Abyss</u>,
an <u>Infinity of Nothingness</u> ("ABZU").

ANCIENT SUMERIAN DEFINITIONS.

<u>ABZU</u> = "Abyss" ("Nothingness")
<u>ZU</u> = "Spiritual Life" ("Awareness")
<u>ANKI</u> = "All Existences" ("Existence")
<u>AN</u> = "Spiritual Universe" ("Heaven")
<u>KI</u> = "Physical Universe" ("Earth")

ALTERNATE MARDUKITE NEXGEN
SYSTEMOLOGY DEFINITIONS.

<u>ABZU</u> = "Infinity of Nothingness"
<u>ZU</u> = "Awareness of Alpha Spirit"
<u>ANKI</u> = "The Standard Model"
<u>AN</u> = "Alpha Existence" ("Spiritual")
<u>KI</u> = "Beta Existence" ("Physical")

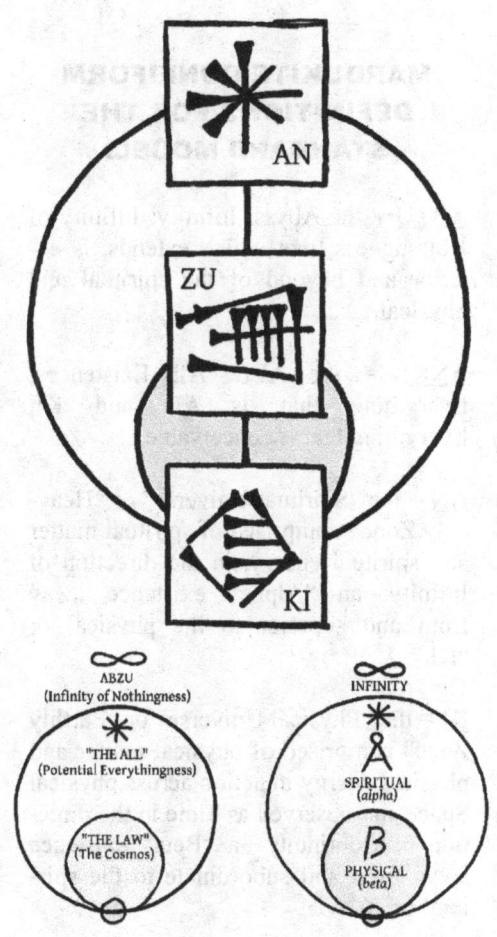

MARDUKITE CUNEIFORM DEFINITIONS FOR THE STANDARD MODEL.

<u>ABZU</u> = the Abyss; Infinity; Infinity of Nothingness; that which extends, is exterior and beyond of the spiritual and physical.

<u>ANKI</u> = the ALL; All Existences; Everything that is AN and KI; Everything that is conceivable.

<u>AN</u> = the "Spiritual Universe" or "Heavenly Zone" comprised of spiritual matter and spiritual energy, in the direction of Infinity—an "Alpha" existence away from and superior to the physical or "KI."

<u>KI</u> = the "Physical Universe" or "Earthly Zone" comprised of physical matter and physical energy in action across physical Space and observed as Time in the direction of Continuity—a "Beta" existence away from and subordinate to the spiritual or "AN."

ZU = "to know"; "knowingness"; "Awareness" or "consciousness"; spiritual energy and matter of AN that is observed as "Lifeforce" in KI; "Spiritual Life Energy"; the actual personal spiritual Identity or "Awareness" of Self as Spirit which extends along a "line" from the Spiritual Universe (AN) to the Physical Universe (KI).

THE TABLETS OF DESTINY & BABYLONIAN CREATION EPIC.

The Absolute behind ALL Existence is referred to on the *Tablets of Destiny* as the Infinity of Nothingness. It is the only constant static of latent unmanifest potentiality of ALL and Everythingness.

The LAW—Cosmic Law—is defined as the Cosmic Dragon—TIAMAT—on "Epic of Creation" Tablets. She is the First Cause or movement across a "Sea of Infinity." Later, the LAW becomes a division between Spiritual Existence ("AN") and any Physical Universe ("KI"). The LAW—Tiamat—permeating ALL, uses the *Tablets of Destiny* and then fixes the systems of finite potential: The Systems of Manifestation—Substance, Motion and Awareness.

"Before heaven or earth are named," the formation and interaction of active existences —"substances" and "bodies" and "Life" and "gods"—creates turbulence and waves of action through space. The governing system of Cosmic Law—Tiamat—responds accordingly. She fixes the Tablets of Destiny to her "deputy"—a messenger wave action of the LAW named "Kingu" and sends him rippling out to "meet" the Anunnaki "gods."

The Anunnaki Assembly of "gods" prepare to battle The LAW. When none among them comes forth to engage, it is the Anunnaki "god" MARDUK that volunteers as hero to confront Kingu and Tiamat—but with a condition that the Anunnaki Assembly recognize him as "Chief of the Gods" upon his success.

When MARDUK approaches the LAW directly, he is flanked by Kingu and the "army of Ancient Ones." MARDUK is able to relinquish the Tablets of Destiny from Kingu. With the Tablets of Destiny, Marduk conquers a true understanding of Cosmic Law and thereby Tiamat.

THE TABLETS OF DESTINY & SELF-HONESTY.

Marduk uses the Tablets of Destiny to discover "Self-Honesty" and Divine Knowledge governing "Cosmic Ordering"—systems dividing the "Spiritual Universe" (AN) from a "Physical Universe" (KI). The two universes are connected only by a stream of Spiritual Lifeforce Awareness that Sumerians called ZU. Wisdom from the Arcane Tablets is later passed down to and concealed by an ancient esoteric secret society in Babylon: the Scribes, High Priests and Priestesses of Mardukite Zuism.

Self-Honesty is a term describing an original "Alpha" state of clear knowingness and Self-directed beingness. "Self-Honesty" is the most basic and true expression of Self as "I-AM"—free of artificial attachments; reactive-response conditioning; and imposed or enforced programming as Reality for the Human Condition. Spiritual development in modern *Mardukite Zuism* is referred to as the "Pathway to Self-Honesty" and the "Gateway to Infinity." It is modeled directly from the Ancient Mystery Tradition observed at the Temples of Babylon.

THE KEY TO THE GATE.

"I will take my Blood—and with Bone—I will fashion a Race of Humans to keep Watch of the Gate. And from the Blood of Kingu I will create another Race of Humans to inhabit the Earth in service to the Gods—so shrines to the Anunnaki may be built and the temples filled. I will bind the Elder Gods to the Watchtowers; let them keep watch over the Gate of Abzu and the Gate of Tiamat and Gate of Kingu—and with a Key that shall be ever hidden, known to none, except only to my Mardukites." —MARDUK, *Enuma Elis, Creation Tablet VI.*

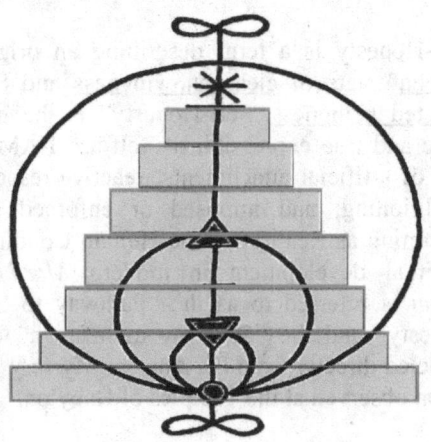

THE ANUNNAKI LADDER OF LIGHTS & BABYLONIAN GATEWAYS TO INFINITY.

ZIGGURAT TEMPLES in Babylonia—and throughout Mesopotamia—served to remind populations of the ZU connecting "Heaven" and "Earth."

Seven-stepped "levels" of the physical ZIG-GURAT TEMPLES of Babylonia—and seven corresponding Gates—represent spiritual levels of actualized Awareness; states of Self-purification (or "spiritual defragmentation") as they ascend in the direction of AN toward Infinity of Supreme Beingness—the Pathway of Self-Honesty—in imitation of the footsteps of the gods during their descent through the "spheres" or "Gates."

COSMOLOGY AND METAPHYSICS.

All Things in the Physical Universe are in motion—wave motions of "energy and matter in space measured as-and-across time." Continuity of the Physical Universe (KI) is divided by LAW and encompassed by the ALL (ANKI).

The direction of AN extends toward ABZU, an Infinity of Nothingness beyond effective existence.

The true <u>Alpha Self</u> is a source—the "spiritual cause" of "physical effects." It engages a <u>Self-determined WILL</u> from its "spiritual" <u>Alpha existence</u> to actualize Awareness for "physical" <u>Beta existence</u> experience as "Life."

USING ANCIENT WISDOM TO UNLOCK HUMAN POTENTIAL.

Communication of clear wisdom and true knowledge from Arcane Tablets is distorted as it passes through time and geography, diverse languages and authoritarian cultures using the "Power" to program the masses and fragment the Human Condition away from Self-Honesty.

Use of this ancient wisdom reveals the Keys to "<u>Cosmic Ordering</u>"—applying the highest Self-directed understanding of "cause-and-effect" sequences in the Physical Universe.

MARDUKITE ZUISM, SYSTEMOLOGY & SPIRITUALITY.

The Spiritual Universe (AN)—of metaphysical or spiritual energy and metaphysical or spiritual matter is not dependent on the Physical Universe (KI) to exist; the two are existentially independent of each other, maintaining a single channel, conduit or connection, which is Alpha Spirit "Awareness" as Spiritual Life or ZU. The Alpha Spirit engages a ZU-line, a spiritual lifeline of ZU energy to a genetic vehicle or organic body to experience physical beta existence.

MARDUKITE ZUISM DEFINITIONS FOR SYSTEMOLOGY.

ALPHA SPIRIT = a spiritual lifeform; the True Self or "I-AM"; the spirit that is controlling the physical body or "genetic vehicle" using a Lifeline or continuum of spiritual "ZU" energy.

ASCENSION = actualized Awareness elevated to (AN) spiritual existence that is exterior to beta-existence.

BETA-EXISTENCE = manifestation in the Physical Universe (KI); the state of existence or condition of frequency specific to physical energy and physical matter in physical space.

FRAGMENTATION = breaking into parts; fractioning wholeness; fracture of holism; discontinuity; separation; outside the state of Self-Honesty.

GENETIC VEHICLE = a physical life-form; the physical (beta) body controlled by the (Alpha) Spirit using a continuous Lifeline of ZU energy.

HUMAN CONDITION = a default programmed conditioned state standard issue Human existence/experience.

ZU-LINE = a spectrum of Spiritual Life-Energy (ZU); an energetic channel or Identity-Continuum connecting Alpha Spirit Awareness from Infinity-to-Infinity including the full physical beta range.

THE HIGHEST FORM OF
TRUE DIVINE WORSHIP.

The true Destiny of Humanity is to achieve spiritual <u>Self-Actualization</u>; the reunion of Self with the Divine. Attaining Self-Honesty in this Life is the most important step a person can take toward achieving their highest ideals, goals and realizations.

The Highest form of "True Worship" begins with the Spirit—the true Self—and all external practices, rituals, ceremonies and historical examples are but outer reflections of this ideal. The Highest form of "Sin" is against the Spirit —against the Self—and its ability to maintain Self-Honesty. There are modes of thought, action and Self-direction of effort that will contribute toward Ascension; and modes that lead away from that.

Beta experiences of "Sin"—pain, fear, guilt, anger—are all related to personal fragmentation; and emotional turbulence from all of these may be released—and intention energy redirected— because: <u>we are all co-creators of Reality in this lifetime!</u>

SPHERES OF EXISTENCE, INFLUENCE & UTILITARIAN ETHICS OF SYSTEMOLOGY.

The prime directive of all beta existence is: *to exist*. The continuation of existence is the purpose behind all existence. Between realization of Self and Infinity, there are many spheres of existence that we may influence. All of the spheres are interconnected.

There is nothing in existence that is in absolute exclusion to all existence. Each sphere of existence supports subsequent existences and assists reaches toward higher spheres of influence.

The greatest good contributes to the greatest continuation of optimum existence for the greatest sphere of inclusion. Degrees of rightness and wrongness are determined by Cosmic Law and are reflected in the quality of, and continuation of, an optimal existence at the highest sphere of existence.

Individual happiness is attained via the channel to the highest sphere. Human unhappiness is the result of "selfishness" and/or lack of "spiritual Self-Actualization" and "Awareness."

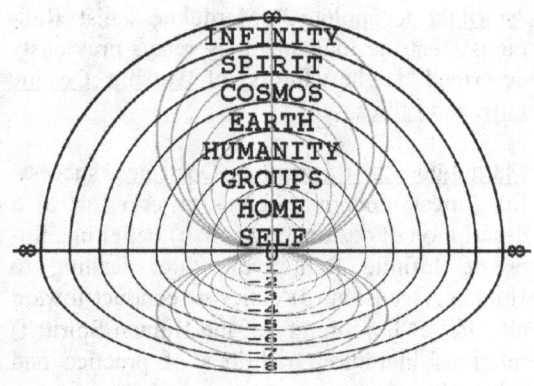

INFINITY
SPIRIT
COSMOS
EARTH
HUMANITY
GROUPS
HOME
SELF

ZU : MARDUKITE ZUISM & MODERN ZUIST RELIGION.

History demonstrates how dangerous, trouble-some and easily misused the concept of "REL-GION" is; so, for purposes of incorporating Mardukite Zuism as a contemporary standard, the idea of "religion" is here treated as:

a concise spiritual paradigm, set of be-liefs and practices, regarding Divinity, Infinite Beingness—or else "God."

Mardukite Zuism operates under a premise of very specific beliefs and a "systemology" of "spiritual technology." Mardukite Zuist Religious Doctrine fundamentally relays previously described "Highest forms" of Worship, Cosmic Law, and Ethics.

Mardukite Zuist Spiritual Doctrines successfully meet modern religious criteria for: a) a description of cosmic creation; b) belief in a Supreme Infinite Being; c) ethics leading to Human Ascension; d) ethics of conduct toward all Life; e) Immortality of the Human Spirit; f) religious literature, traditions of practice and spiritual advisement.

GOALS & IDEALS OF MARDUKITE ZUISM.

The word "ZU" meant "knowing" in original Sumerian cuneiform script. Goals and ideals of Zuism reflect this. Mardukite Zuism seeks to assist an individual in reclaiming a realization of the True Self or "I-AM" as the Immortal Spirit, in line with a most ancient directive: to "Know Thyself."

In view of the fact that all modern humans are subjected to technologies depriving them of their freedoms to *be, think, know* and pursue truth: the goals and ideals of Zuism are to effectively revive and repair these very abilities and certainties of the Individual—as an increase of "Actualized Awareness."

INFINITY, "GOD" & SUPREME BEINGNESS

The Spiritual Philosophy of Zuism is systematized by a Standard Model. It demonstrates Absolute Supreme Beingness associated with the Highest realization of "God" as INFINITY. No thing is Higher or Absolute than the Infinity of Nothing—and reducing Supreme Beingness to any finite personality or character trait is to limit and defile with lesser "words."

The Highest Name of God cannot be conceived —hence our symbolic use of the Infinity Sign:

∞

...or Sumerian cuneiform word-sign: "ABZU" —"The Infinite Nothingness and Source of All ZU."

The Spiritual Universe (AN) is *All-as-One* because it exists as an infinite singularity or stasis:

infinite potential with no gradient or observed motion; which is its own continuity.

The Physical Universe (KI) is *All-as-One* because it is in continuous motion, with all manifest parts working systematically as a continuity of beta-existence.

A "spiritual continuum" or "conduit channel" of ZU—absolute energy from the Spiritual Universe (AN)—links our Awareness levels of "I-AM," "True Self" or Spirit ("Alpha Spirit") with the degrees of motion and variation in the Physical Universe.

This Alpha Spirit or "Soul" is the true Awareness, "I" or "Self" connected to the operation and control of the physical body.

THE TRUE HUMAN ALPHA SPIRIT.

The true Self is the "I" or "Spirit" regardless of its position, degree or level of Awareness. Spirit remains. Whatever "spiritual energy-matter" composes the Alpha Spirit or "soul"—it must occupy this "other space" with its spiritual existence and then project its Awareness and Will onto the Physical Universe (KI) in order to experience the Game we call Life.

This "spiritual energy-matter" that composes all Life (as a Lifeforce with Awareness and Consciousness) goes by many names throughout history—but we find the idea first treated as <u>ZU</u> on cuneiform tablets of Mesopotamia.

On an Identity lifeline of ZU energy, all Alpha Spirits are operating from a Spiritual Universe. We refer to this as the ZU-line on the Standard Model.

ZU is the name given to the spiritual essence of all Life in existence—and Self is a concentrated center or focal point as a ZU-continuum or Identity.

The True Self of an Individual Human is a "spiritual universe cause" of "physical universe effects"—engaging as an immortal Alpha Spirit with a Self-determined Will actualized as an Awareness along the ZU-continuum, extending from Infinity-to-Infinity, through every possible frequency and vibration along the total spectrum of physical and metaphysical existence.

THE SYSTEMOLOGY PRACTICES OF SPIRITUAL ADVISEMENT & COUNSELING SERVICES FOR MARDUKITE ZUISM.

The Mardukite Chamberlains were established in 2009 dedicated to recovery and consolidation of all historical, scriptural & ritual records of ancient Babylon in Mesopotamia. In 2011, a Mardukite faction (International Systemology Society) began to research and develop methods to apply ancient wisdom as a futurist spiritual technology that awakens, unlocks and fully actualizes spiritual potential of the Human Condition.

A systematic approach to spirituality is seen on the Standard Model, where ZU-line frequencies are represented at various degrees: "zero-point" body death; cellular activity and sensory perceptions of a genetic body; bio-chemicals induced by emotion; thoughts and intention transmitted between our Alpha Spirit and the "genetic vehicle"—all the way "up" the scale to a perfected clarity of Self-Actualized Awareness of I-AM as our true "Alpha" state, just below Infinity and Absolute Beingness.Full potential of ZU in Consciousness is only altered from its natural state as a result of personal fragmentation of the Human Condition. This may be restored with spiritual practices.

The Pathway to Self-Honesty is a personal journey and spiritual adventure marked by progressive clearing of spiritual energy channels fragmented by the imprinting and programming accumulated from experiences in our environment—the "debris" that fragments the total actualized experience of Self in Awareness as the Alpha Spirit.

The first and most important step—Before an individual can actualize potentials of the Spirit as Self, they must fully realize: the I-AM Self and the Alpha Spirit are One.

This state of Knowingness is the primary intention of basic spiritual practices found in Mardukite Zuism.

"Systemology" books and advanced training courses are also available to Mardukite Ministers seeking to qualify as specialized clergy, priests, priestess, and systematic processing pilots.

CREED OF MARDUKITE ZUISM.
PRINCIPLES OF BELIEF.*

1.) We believe in an Absolute Beingness, which is Infinite—the ABZU—the All-as-One encompassing Source of All Being, Knowing and Awareness to all Alpha (Spiritual-AN) and Beta (Physical-KI) states of existence.

2.) We believe in a spiritual energy of all Life and Awareness—ZU—in the physical universe (beta) that is an effect of a spiritual (Alpha) cause; a Spirit that is cause. This Spirit—in its Alpha state—is the True Self "I-AM" Individual Identity that many have called the "soul."

3.) We believe that the Human Condition is a genetic vehicle used by a spiritual source (AN) to experience the Finite as physical existence (KI)—that we are Awareness (ZU) projected onto a genetic vehicle—and that while the vehicle/body may perish to physical entropy, the "Alpha Spirit" remains immortal and Self-directed to the extent of its own Actualized Awareness.

---

* First drafted in 2019.

4.) We believe that the highest form of worship and spirituality is the actualization and advancement of our "Self" as Spirit in Self-Honesty—and that Self-Honesty is the I-AM Alpha state of Being and Knowing, which is realizable in this lifetime.

5.) We believe that the purpose of all existence is: to exist—and that the prime directive of all spiritual Life is: continued existence of spiritual Life and co-creation of habitable Reality. "Good" and "Moral" actions are evaluated to the extent of this end.

6A.) We believe that no Life exists in exclusion to all other Life—and that the conditions of a habitable Reality extending from Self include:
Home; Community; All Humanity; All Life on Earth; All Life in the Universe; All Spiritual Life; and the Infinite.

6B.) We believe in a continued evolution of Alpha Spirit awareness developed beyond one physical life, and that a Spirit experiences many.

7A.) We believe Mardukite Zuism and its applied systemology is a 21st Century AD synthesis of the 21st Century BC wisdom collected on cuneiform tablets and experienced in ancient Mesopotamia, esp. Babylon.

7B.) This cuneiform library included details concerning: beings called the Anunnaki; ordering of the Cosmos; creation of Humanity; and an entire legacy of systematized traditions.

8.) We believe in the continuation of, and proper communication of, the true legacy of Human history—and the ability of every Human to realize that they are a Free Spirit in a Free Zone of Self-Determinism: and no "evils" can affect intentions if an individual is spiritually Self-Actualized in Self-Honesty.

THE ARCANE KNOWLEDGE FROM MARDUK'S TABLET OF DESTINY.*

1.) As above, so below;
On earth as it is in Heaven
an-bala ki-bala an-ba ki an-ba

2.) What the Mind believes, the Spirit reinforces
da-ga nam-ku-zu dingir-Lamma a bi-ib-gar

3.) When disaster is self-made,
no man can interfere
*nig-ku-lam-ma dingir-ra-na-ka su—
tu-tu nu-ub-zu*

4.) What is given in submission
is a catalyst for defiance
nig-gu-gar-ra nig-gaba-gar-ra

5.) Whoever partners with Truth, creates Life
nig-ge-na-ta a-ba in-da-di nam-ti i-u-tu

---

* Excerpted from *"Tablets of Destiny"* by Joshua Free.

THE

MAQLU

RITUAL BOOK

A collection of the most ancient
historical cuneiform ritual records
accounting for the Maqlu Ritual.
Being a series of incantations
to the Order of Nabu, scribe-priests,
magicians and priestesses of Babylon;
a ceremonial sequence of counterspells,
exorcisms and protective rites
in honor of the Anunnaki pantheon.

MAQLU EXORCISMS & BANISHINGS
(MARDUKITE M-SERIES ARCHIVE)*

Here is the *Book of Burnt Offerings*, the *Book of Burnings*, and *Book of Exorcisms* handed down from the Keepers of the Old Ways—when ENKI walked the Earth, and made his home in *Eridu*. Here is the *Book of Maqlu Tablets*—key components to the ancient mysteries of "Mardukite" Babylonian Tradition as given to the priests of NABU and MARDUK. When the practitioner finds times of warfare not of this world—when malignant energies run rampant—when the wicked witch and warlock cast their evil magick against thee by the grace of their gods—in such times of trial, a self-honest Priest or Priestess of the *Anunnaki* is not left unprotected.

Functional use of ceremonial exorcisms to banish "evil spirits" is a most ancient form of mysticism —and "sympathetic magic"—perhaps the oldest of all forms. On a personal level, the purpose of the "*Maqlu*" (or "*Maklu*") cuneiform tablet series is exoterically—or outwardly and commonly understood—to target "evil spirits" and "evil-doers" (called "witch" or "warlock") that either has attacked or is actively working against the magician, their family and/or community.

---

*   Mardukite Catalogue = *Tablet M*

As a petition for the "power of the gods," it is assumed that the enemy operates their existence of Self within a similar *Anunnaki* cultural "paradigm" (worldview) and that the more righteous and pious servant of this tradition need only appeal to the same energetic authorities by which to shut the enemy off from their source—and in extreme situations, resulting in the fitful death of the enemy, and at the very least, a means of protecting the practitioner from any further assaults.

THE BOOK OF MAQLU & MAQLU RITUAL.

The Mardukite Tablet-M or "*Maqlu*" series consists of nine Akkadian-Babylonian cuneiform tablets illustrating a very extensive ritual—or combination of several rituals and incantations—by which the "Priest" (magician, practitioner, priestess, &tc.) calls on the power of Chief Gods from the *Anunnaki* pantheon: *Anu, Enlil, Enki, Marduk* and *Shammash* to "curse," "banish," "exorcise"— or literally "burn"—all of the evil-doers and wickedness of society in an elaborate ceremonial effort. Such rites were even held publicly as a major national festival event.

We translate the word "*Maqlu*"—or "*Maklu*" if you still prefer to subscribe to the "Simon" semantics—to mean "burnings," indicative of the type of effigy scape-goat "witch-burnings" envisioned from the Middle Ages, except for one key difference: _no_ living beings are burned or sacrificed for the ritual. "*Maqlu*" ceremonial "effigy" burnings are metaphoric—rooted in sympathetic magic—performed with "images" of your enemy, symbolic representations of all the evil plaguing society.

THE DARK ARTS OF BABYLON.*

How often we have heard of the "Dark Arts" born of a "polarized" and "dualistic" view of the universe—and *forces* that occupy it. It is a simple order of things—for every pious priestly "magician," there is a dark spell against him; and to every system of *Order*, there is a *Chaos* factor—no fragmented experience of reality can ever actually exist isolated in perfect "balance." There is the pendulum swing of action and the movement of energy throughout the cosmos amorally controlling the tidal ebb and flow of universal currents. This is what makes energetic activity of "creation" or "manifestation" possible in the "physical world"— or at least our perception of a "3-Dimensional" reality experienced. As such, with a once united "crystal" being cracked into varied refractions of human experience, language and culture, a "dualistic" world also emerged early in human consciousness; right before the very eyes of ancient

---

* Mardukite Catalogue = *Liber-M; Tablet M*

Mesopotamians—from the heart and cradle of known human civilization.

It is not within the scope of the current "*Liber-M*" archives to put forth an entire basis for the ancient *Anunnaki* tradition—or to catalogue the numerous historic *firsts* that arose from *Sumerian* culture "as if from nowhere"—or the greater legacy of post-Sumerian "Mardukite" *Babylon* throughout the evolution of human civilization, societal order, "belief systems" and their long-standing and far-sweeping effects on the planet and its populations. All of this has already been so concisely organized and offered in previous materials form the "Mardukite" literary collection. For our present purposes, we fix our sights on a specific singular element within all of this—the "Maqlu" cuneiform tablet series pertaining to the "Dark Arts" as encountered in the ancient *Mardukite* system observed in *Babylon*.

As a method of ancient spirituality realized through "ritual magic," this newly revised and translated "*Maqlu*" text is comprehensible as introduced and presented—though it is suggested that the reader-seeker or potential practitioner is familiar with the greater scope of Mesopotamian or "Mardukite Babylonian" tradition that these rites are derived from. "Magic" of this system is considered *high magic* and *holy magic* once reserved to an intellectually and spiritually elite class of priests and priestesses in Babylon—dependent on an *established* true and faithful relationship between the "operator" and the "supreme" powers ceremonially called forth.

Esoteric books transcribe excerpts of early academic "Maqlu" incantation translations out of context and tend to emphasize the more "colorful" elements portrayed by the tradition—those most appropriately pertaining to Dark Arts: "Sumerian Sorcery," "Babylonian Witchcraft," "Mesopotamian Exorcisms," "magickal warfare" or "wizards' duels." The full picture shared via the Mardukite "Liber-M"/"M-Series" interpretive materials and translations offers an entirely new a more complete rendering of this 4,000+ year old operation from esoteric experimentation by the "Mardukite Research Organization" conducted from 2009 through 2019.

* * * * * * *

Mesopotamian languages are archaic forms of communication that we are still only now reaching clear understandings of. Yet—as with many terms —the words may often be interpreted differently, and it is not uncommon for meanings to shift during information transmission based on variegated perceptions, literal language differences, semantic issues and even personal beliefs of the translators. That being said: typically understand MAQLU to mean "*the Burnings*." This context is a good *base* for our working knowledge of the rites—especially in public displays of a community bonded together to "burn evil in effigy." It is even possible that the term more accurately describes a "*burning man*" if we adopt a similar literal interpretation of *maq-lu*.

The complete "*Maqlu*" operation evolved from what was once probably a much simpler, mostly internalized, meditative and solitary protection ritual used by the earliest priests, priestesses and magicians in *Mesopotamia*. It later developed more dramatically as a public "*Fire Festival*" in Sumer and Babylonia, involving entire community populations gathered together in combined mass focuses of emotional and spiritual intention to "drive out" or *dispel* "evil" and "evil-doers" of the land. Here we see an ancient demonstration in effective abilities of mass-consciousness moving energies when large groups—or better, the majority of the population—focuses on a specific "emotional" event. Even as "quantum" events, the social effects carry very real ramifications for the consciousness of the population—and perhaps the greater cosmos as a whole in this entangled universe. So long as the event is properly orchestrated, the individuals need not even be aware of the exact esoteric nature of their participation.

Ritual incantations from "*Maqlu*" tablets coincide with construction and incineration of representative images—the *Burning Man* symbolizing all the "evil-doers" of the world—those "plaguing" humanity with their wickedness, thereby upsetting the "world order" of the *gods*, in addition to the *gods* themselves—those Anunnaki figures sharing a covenant of protection with their pious priests and priestesses.

The upset of a disharmonic balance was usually felt throughout the community socially as "illness" and "pestilence," "disease" and "famine"—and such could prove devastating to a still developing human civilization. Actions leading toward such malignant results were deemed "evil" and often personified as the most wicked of "demons." Anything that might lead to unhealthy results—mostly concerning uncleanliness and misappropriated living—were considered "taboo," else the original tribal "sins," and for good reason. For example— eating from an unclean plate was "taboo" (a "sin") because it could lead to the spread of disease. Clearly, ancient humans were meticulous observers far from *primitive* in their understanding of the natural world and their relationship with it. Before political authoritarian use in classical times, "taboos" and "sins" were not given from dogma—but out of medicinal necessity. Humans were not "civilized" by nature; they were "trained"—and language, civic systems and "priestly institutions" developed to oversee this, maintain it, and even enforce it.

* * * * * * *

Representative "images" have a long-standing history of use in "idol magic" or "sympathetic magic." These are not instruments of demonic worship—as some mythographers have repeatedly put forth—but are instead symbolic embodiments of an "energetic current." These energies are universally entangled to a "focal object" and its form—and by the laws of "sympathetic magic," affecting the form can equally affect the same universally entangled energies it represents. We see this in other similar methods that are enacted to affect a person from a distance by using something that belongs to them, or better still: hair, nail clippings, and so forth. In related practices of necromancy and ancestral magic, personal articles and bone fragments are similarly used as relics to connect to a specific "entangled" energy from across the astral.

"Sympathetic magic" appears strongly in *Maqlu* rituals numerous times where a representative *image* of "evil," a "demon," a "wicked witch" or "evil warlock" is constructed and then ceremonially obliterated. These "idols" are not subjects of worship or glorification of Babylonian "daemonology," but to demonstrate control over—or at the very least, the ability to appeal to the Anunnaki gods that maintain control over—the chaotic forces of the universe that are often perverted by the wicked toward selfish and antagonistic ends.

The *images* represent known and unknown "enemies of the state," or in more personal cases, a "witch" or "warlock" who is using magic against you. The degree of cosmic coherence portrayed by the entire "*Maqlu*" ceremony is far from primitive.

* * * * * * *

It is next to impossible to conjure a metaphysical or esoteric conversation of the "*Burning Man*" to a "New Age" mind without also considering more geographically and chronologically recent examples from the Western world. One that even motion pictures have made into a household name is derived from Roman-inspired writings concerning the *Celtic Druids*—called the *Wicker Man*, or else the "Burning Man" by some neopagans and others who revive emotionally-purging cathartic annual festivals even today. Although once incited as part of ancient warfare and even fertility rites, modern celebrations of community and healthy artistic release actually mirror original "mass consciousness" esoteric festivals very closely.

As a magical component, *Fire* commonly appears in "magical" and "shamanic" systems during early development of human civilization—in fact, mastery of *Fire* indisputably correlates *with* development of modern humans. Antiquated "*Fire Festivals*" are aligned to the *Sun*—often appearing to coincide with critical turning points of the year, an annual cycle marked by key points of agricultural significance: the planting and harvest of sustaining foodstuffs.

"Light" and "dark" halves of the year also marked points of spiritual significance, such as we see with the Akiti/Akitu Babylonian New Year observed on the Spring Equinox—a turning point that celebrates renewal of the realm. Opposite this festival of "lights" we also observe a "darker" time of year, ritually dramatized as a cyclic mythological *struggle* between *order* and *chaos*, *creation* and *entropy*, *life* and *death*—and to ensure the pendulum swing returns to the side of *Life*, we are given personal and communal "purification" exercises—the "*Maqlu*."

The "*Maqlu*" ritual is sometimes called the "*Rite of Burnt Offerings*" because—using consecrated "images" charged with intention and heavy emotional energy—the "soul" of evil, or "souls" of evil-doers, are destroyed or "sacrificed" by incineration to benefit the world and a prosperous nation. Modern "revival" practitioners within "Mardukite" tradition and other systems of Mesopotamian "neo-paganism" have found varying degrees of success using popular translations of these exorcism tablets. That success increases exponentially and synchronously with the practitioner's understanding and experience with both "practical magic" (including "mysticism") and an understanding of *Anunnaki* "systemology"—the core knowledge base found throughout the modern "Mardukite" library of materials.

Much of the "Mesopotamian Magic" tradition is contained within archaic cuneiform religious or incantation tablets, and the "*Maqlu*" tablet series is no exception. However, these incantations are supplemented with specific ceremonial actions—the construction and consecration of various "images of the enemy" and ritual gestures describing the manner of cursing and incineration by fire: the "burnings."

Esoterically, public observance of "*Maqlu*" rites allowed for a shift in mass consciousness—the triumphant night of "order conquering chaos" reminiscent of European "Halloween" rites. Meanwhile, for the priesthood, the "*Maqlu*" ritual is a serious "astral ceremony" in which the practitioner would "climb the *Ladder of Lights*" and appeal to the Anunnaki gods for personal protection, the protection of the city (community), and destruction (elimination) of the enemy to this "world order"— all evil-doers and wicked witches and warlocks throughout the lands operating intently against the community. As a fixed movement of large directed amounts of energy, the ceremony enacts a "chain-curse" projected outward to extend far and beyond the immediate environment as a "public service" meant to "purge" the Realm.

A practical execution of the *"Maqlu"* ritual in its entirety requires intensive concentration—the full focus and adept attention of a practicing magician or priestess, perhaps in excess of a day, as the full observation is an overnight firelit vigil of ceremonial "cleansing" and emotional "purging" for the community—the most ancient "Burning Man" festival. Although not indicated on the *"Maqlu"* tablets themselves, all of the traditional ritual elements—preparation of the *Temple*, evoking *Guardians of the Watchtowers* and invoking the *Anunnaki* gods and their spiritual *Star Gates of Babylon*—are carefully observed before conducting any of the numerous *"Maqlu"* incantation-rituals. Supporting information is also relayed throughout the greater literary collection of modern "Mardukite" materials contained within the present anthology.

MAQLU MAGIC.

Esoteric "New Age" revival of *Maqlu* fragments for *Simon's Necronomicon* left many early initiates to wonder what *more* might remain behind the curtains of this form of Babylonian mysticism. In fact, even among the "Mardukite Research Organization," a full translation and total understanding of the complete ceremony would take nearly a decade amidst other work. Naturally, *Simon's Necronomicon* offered only a small part of the *Maqlu* data, just as we have seen in examples from many modern Mardukite predecessors—a greater literary cycle and spiritual tradition exists beneath the surface interpretations that have gone on inspiring for decades. Within and about all of the complete *Maqlu* cuneiform tablet series we find nothing short of a purely "Mardukite Babylonian" masterpiece of authentic ceremonial ritualism.

Many esoteric readers were first introduced to the *Maqlu* (or "*Maklu*") from the elementary and bastardized fragments appearing in the *Simon* work—causing many to overlook, dismiss or confuse what the original cuneiform *Maqlu* tablets actually represent. Only a small portion of the complete text appears in the popular *Simon* edition, and they are treated as individual rites of protective "counter-magic" against "worshipers of the *Ancient Ones*" and not as a singular ceremonial expression.

There are other common elements of the *Maqlu* incantations that occultists and esoteric magicians find reminiscent to other mystical work in related systems: *Arabic, Semitic, Assyrian, Canaanite, Hebrew, &tc.* In such comparisons, similar incantations appear in forms of "healing magic" or to drive away "evil spirits"—what we refer to as "*exorcisms.*" More than simply combating entities and energies directly, the *Maqlu* magic focuses on practitioners feeding these power-currents their existence (via participation and belief). At the same time, these "evil worshipers" are feeding off of and deriving channeled energy from malignant currents appearing "negative" in polarity when clashed against the "reality" of the ordered "Realm."

Maqlu magic stands apart uniquely, even amidst a modern "New Age" revival of ancient esoterica. Similar practices held by "politically correct occultism" of today are mainly *passive* "binding" meditations employing only the "astral powers *of the shield*." The *Maqlu* offers ancient priest-magicians of the "State" a means of "magical law enforcement" with "astral powers *of the sword*." As a religious practice, the *Maqlu* enables the pious priest and priestess mystic rights to "fight fire" with "God-Fire."

BABYLONIAN MAGIC & WITCHCRAFT.

Ancient magical practice and beliefs—as external demonstrations of will and outward ritualized communion with the "cosmos"—are common throughout the ancient world, and no less so in the underground today. Practice of magic, in and of itself, was not criminal in Mesopotamia—a cultural region adept in its widespread use and even producing a tradition known today as the *Chaldean Magi*—from which we have our word "magician." This being said: "magic" was an institution of the "State"—or that is to say, linked specifically to systematic power of the "Realm." Esoteric incantation tablets were sole property of "official" scribe-priests, priestess, magicians and kings of the "Realm." To be clear: few citizens outside this elite circle were even literate enough to read them.

The original magical traditions were exclusively observed by those in positions of civic responsibility, those charged by a "Divine Right"—the covenant of *Anunnaki gods*—to appropriately execute esoteric "magical arts" throughout the realm. These were dispensed alongside a more "outward" (*exoteric*) "religious" understanding carried by the general masses. This distinction in understanding is reflected even today among the esoteric "Mardukite" movement in contrast to a purely academic or historic pursuit of Mesopotamian mysteries without adherence to the authentic paradigm or systemology that the material is derived from. Clearly, what is generally available to *seekers* now —after thousands of years of fragmentation, cultural separation, paradigm formations and other various *grimoires*—is but a *shadow* of the "real magic" secretly known to the ancient mystics working side-by-side with their Anunnaki "*Sky Gods.*"

Misinformed efforts, by later humans, corrupted the "sacred arts" of *magic*. But, this is not about placing blame; it matters little *who* is at fault now —only that the issue is rectified. The ancient mystics considered "priestly-magic" as "divine" or "transcendental," given to the *"Race of Marduk"* as a birth-right; *sacred* and not to be taken for granted. Education and use of "magical arts" were a closely guarded secret among the most ancient factions, sects and schools—all connected to *Anunnaki* traditions in whatever guises and names they might carry, or by whatever language or semantics they apply to the same universal system. Many later schools—later branches of the tree— were far removed, fragmented and divided from the original source, leaving each of the various sects only a limited understanding—a limited perceptual experience—of the *All-as-One*.

When we examine the specific language used throughout the *Maqlu*—and the disapproving labels applied to wicked evil-doers dedicated to the *"Dark Arts"*—the Seeker uncovers origins for a spiritual division or distinction regarding "class magic." Where some portray the *Maqlu* itself as a *"Book of Black Magic,"* this could not be further from the truth. Instead we discover a spiritual and religious method for *fighting*, *countering* and *defending* against the "Dark Arts." What's more— rather than put a self-honest magician at the risk of "turning to the Dark Side" or committing overt acts, the *Maqlu* ritual allows the *Mardukite* to petition *Anunnaki* to execute final judgment and any retribution on their behalf. Of course, the literal nature of the *Maqlu* magic is still considered the "Dark Arts" to an extent—but when used on the side of *right*, karmic and energetic repercussions are transferred away from the operator and taken up by the divine intermediary. By appealing to the "Highest," the one who is in greatest alignment with *cosmic order* will prevail.

In contrast to terms like "priest," "priestess," "magician" or "seer," we see a clear distinction between these pious practitioners and the "wicked witch" or "evil warlock" that they are fighting against using *Maqlu* rituals. This means that the term "witch" has had a negative connotation since the original birth of language in Mesopotamia—not against a gender or practitioner of magic, but as a specific term for one who practices magic "outside" or "apart" from the ordered system of pious "priestly" spirituality. Although seldom relayed accurately by historians and academicians, the entire religious framework and infrastructure of Mesopotamia, Sumer, Babylonia, &tc. is entirely rooted in "Cosmic Order" and living unto the highest accord in alignment with "Cosmic Law" as described by the early Sumeriologist, Samuel N. Kramer, in his book: "*History Begins at Sumer*"—

> "The Sumerians, according to their own records, cherished goodness and truth, law and order, justice and freedom, righteousness and straightforwardness, mercy and compassion. And they abhorred evil and

60

falsehood, lawlessness and disorder, injustice and oppression, sinfulness and perversity, cruelty and pitilessness. Kings and rulers constantly boasted of the fact that they had established law and order in the land; protected the weak from the strong; the poor from the rich; and wiped out evil and violence. . . The gods, too, according to the Sumerian sages, preferred the ethical and moral to the unethical and immoral, and practically all the major deities of the [Anunnaki] pantheon are extolled in Sumerian hymns as lovers of the good and the just, of truth and righteousness. . ."

THE MAQLU RITUAL INSTRUCTIONS.

Using *Mardukite* standards of operation, the *Maqlu* ritual is conducted by "Divine Right" and via the *"Incantation of Marduk,"* which is to say the *"Incantation of the Deep"* or *"Incantation of Eridu."* All *fundamental* elements of "Mardukite" ritual apply. Acknowledgment of the control and authority of Marduk in Babylon is among these— such as described by the scribe-priests of *Nabu* in the *Enuma Elis,* Babylonian *"Creation Tablets"* attributing all worldly authority to the Anunnaki god *Marduk*. It was not uncommon for this "myth" to be told or dramatically reenacted for festival ceremonies, as indicated in the Akiti/Akitu Spring Festival performance instructions.

Maqlu magic operates under the occult doctrine known in anthropology as "sympathetic magic" or "transference." It's based on mystical principles of entanglement and correspondence—often illustrated in the axiom: *Like attracts Like*.

In our original descriptions of the *Maqlu* from previous "Mardukite" literature, the *initiate* is shown the "Ladder of Lights" on which they must "ascend" in order to appeal to the *Anunnaki gods* and make their petition for the occasion. In this instance, the power of *Starfire* or God-Fire ("Fire of God") is called forth and consecrated for a singular lofty purpose—*burning of evil*. Naturally, this priestly authority to command is restricted to those adept initiates already having "traversed" the *Gates of Babylon* and developed a personal relationship with the *Anunnaki gods*.

No definitive description is included with the *Maqlu* tablets proper, but we might surmise that the traditional cloth dressings (of practitioners and the altar, &tc.) appropriate to this type of magic are *black*. However, as traditional priestly garments were *white*, we can assume the practitioner changes their attire during the complete *Maqlu* sequence, probably right after evening "counter-spells" and "exorcisms" are performed and the rites move toward a focus of "purification" and the emerging "dawn" that dispels the darkness. [On a related note, blue and purple hues (often with gold

accents) were also common among elite classes—
later adopted as "royal" colors in Europe.]

Maqlu tablet instructions indicate quite clearly that
this ritual is to be exclusively "performed by the
pure offspring of the Deep," meaning specifically
"Mardukites." The *"Deep"* is a literal translation
for the domain of *E.A.–Enki*, whose domain is the
"Deep" or *"Eridu,"* the ancient home of *Enki*,
where *Marduk* and *Nabu* were apprenticed in the
esoteric, scientific and magical arts of the *Anunnaki*. This same mystery tradition passed to "Mardukites" of Babylon and were eventually pre-
served on cuneiform tablets by priest-scribes dedicated to *Nabu* and the legacy of *Marduk*. Among
the many tablet series offering suggestions for
modern methods of practical magic, we find the
Maqlu.

All traditional "Mardukite Babylonian" ceremonial applications are intended for a "temple" environment, one that is regularly prepared and energet-
ically charged through repeated use in dedication
to the *Anunnaki* pantheon. Naturally, as with all
modern efforts toward ancient esoteric revitaliza-
tion and rekindling, there are obviously many
ways of adapting the original methods for portabil-
ity and practicality. In the instance where a physical permanent temple-space is not maintained, we
find many cuneiform tablet examples suggesting a
mandala of sorts—elsewhere referred to in West-

ern occultism as *casting a circle*. A personal/portable *mandala* or "magic circle" is called *usurtu* on some cuneiform tablets and this sacred space was often distinguished by a circle, glyphs and other symbols marked on the ground with consecrated "Grain-flour of Nabu" (called "Flour of Nisaba" in more antiquated Sumerian examples). A few Mesopotamian texts also refer to sprinkling lime throughout the internal

The *"Burnt Offerings"* are constructed according to the materials described on *Maqlu* tablets. This newly revised edition restores this information corresponding with each incantation that is usually not disclosed until the final (ninth) tablet.

Additional ritual components are consecrated and incorporated as indicated throughout the text, but it is evident that a supply of specific materials for fashioning images are prepared ahead of time. Additionally, one is to make all petitions to the *Anunnaki* pantheon "before an image of your god and goddess," often the patrons of a particular city or priestly sect. In Babylon, popular images of *Marduk* and *Sarpanit* (and even *Nabu* and *Teshmet*) are frequently used in religious ceremonies, such as during the Akiti/Akitu festival (see *Liber-51/52* given in this anthology). Finally, a reoccurring presence of "seven idol" statues or "seven watchers" often appears on ritual magic tablets of Mesopotamia.

64

[The cuneiform *Maqlu M-Tablet Series* is given in the following section. A transliterated sign for EN and SU.EN marked the beginning and ending of each incantation—allowing us to easily separate each section of the ritual. As these words are not said as part of the verbal incantation, they are not redundantly used in this transcription.]

THE CUNEIFORM

MAQLU

RITUAL TABLETS

THE MAQLU SERIES – TABLET I

OPENING INCANTATION—PETITION TO THE GODS.

al-si-ku-nu-ši ilimeš mu-ši-ti
I call upon you, Gods of Night
it-ti-ku-nu al-si mu-ši-tum kal-la-tum ku-túm-tum
With you, I call upon the Night, the Veiled Lady
al-si ba-ra-ri-tum qab-li-tum u na-ma-ri-tum
I call at twilight, midnight and dawn,
áš-šú kassaptuú-kaš-šip-an-ni
Because the sorcerer has enchanted me,
[5] e-li-ni-tum ub-bi-ra-an-ni
A [sorceress] has spoken against me,
ili-ia ù distar-ia ú-šis-su-ú eli-ia
Causing my god and goddess to distance from me;
elî a-me-ri-ia am-ru-u a-na-ku
I am a pathetic sight to behold,
im-di-ku la a-la-lu mûša ù ur-ra
I am unable to rest day or night
qu-ú im-ta-na-al-lu-ú pî-ia
and a gag has filled my mouth
[10] ú-pu-un-ti pi-ia ip-ru-su
food has been kept from my mouth
mêmeš maš-ti-ti-ia ú-ma-u-ú
the water ceases to enter my throat;
e-li-li nu-bu-ú hi-du-ti si-ip-di
my praise is lament, my rejoice is sorrow:
i-zi-za-nim-ma ilimeš rabutimeš ši-ma-a da-ba-bi

stand by my side, Great Gods, give me notice,

di-ni di-na a-lak-ti lim-da

be a judge in my case, grant me a decision.

[15] e-pu-uš alam amelkaššapi-ia u kaššapti-ia

I formed an image of my sorcerer and
sorceress,

šá e-piš-ia u muš-te-piš-ti-iar

of my enchanter and enchantress;

áš-kun ina šap-li-ku-nu-ma a-dib-bu-ub di-ni

I have laid them in fire and await your
judgment;

áš-šú i-pu-šá lim-ni-e-ti iš-te-'-a la ba-na-a-ti

because [they] have conjured evil against me:

ši-i li-mut-ma a-na-ku lu-ub-lut

may [they] die, that I can live!

[20] kiš-pu-šá ru-hu-šá ru-sú-u-šá lip-pa-áš-ru

The evil magick, the evil spell must be broken!

ibînu lil-lil-an-ni šá qim-ma-tú ša-ru-ú

The [*Tamarisk*] purifies me!

igišimmaru lip-šur-an-ni ma-hi-rat ka-lu-ú šáru

The [datepalm] catching all the wind, frees me!

šam-maštakal li-bi-ban-ni šá iritimtim ma-la-a-ta

The [*maskatal*] shines through me, filling the
earth.

terînatu lip-šur-an-ni šá še-am ma-la-a-ta

The [pine-cone] full of seeds, frees me!

[25] ina mah-ri-ku-nu e-te-lil ki-ma šamsassati

In front of you I have become light as grass;

e-te-bi-ib az-za-ku ki-ma la-ar-di

I am shinning and pure like grass.

69

tu-ú-šá šá kaššapti li-mut-te
The spell of the [sorceress] is baneful;
tu-ur-rat amât-sa ana pî-šá lišân-šá qa-a-rat
Let [her] words fall in her mouth, tongue-tied!
in elî kiš-pi-šá lim-ha-u-ši ilimeš mu-ši ti
Let the Gods of Night overcome [her] spell.
[30] maarâtimeš šá mu-ši lip-šu-ru ru-hi-šá lim-nu-ti
Let the Three Watchers overcome the evil spell.
pú-šá lu-ú lipû lišân-šá lu-ú âbtu
Let [her] words be dust and tongue turned to salt,
šá iq-bu-ú amât limutimtim-ia ki-ma lipî lit-ta-tuk
which spoke the baneful formula, come to dust!
šá i-pu-šú kiš-pi ki-ma âbti liš-har-mi
The magick, let it dissolve like salt!
qi-is-ru-šá pu-u-u-ru ip-še-tu-šá hul-lu-qú
The knots are undone, [her] efforts are destroyed,
[35] kal a-ma-tu-šá ma-la-a êra
All [her] words fill the void
ina qi-bit iq-bu-ú ilimeš mu-ši-tum
by the covenant that the Gods of Night decreed!

INCANTATION—PETITION TO THE EARTH GODS.
irsitumtum irsitumtum irsitumtum-ma
Earth! Earth! Ye Spirit of the Earth
dgilgameš BEL ma-mi-ti-ku-nu

[Gilgamesh] is the lord of your course!
min-mu-ú at-tu-nu te-pu-šá ana-ku i-di
What has befallen you, I know:
[40] min-mu-ú ana-ku ip-pu-šu at-tu-nu ul ti-da-a
What has befallen me, you know not yet.
min-mu-ú kaššapatimeš-ia ip-pu-šá e-ga-a-pa-ti-ra pa-šir lâ irašši
What the [sorceress] has let loose on me, no one can undo; it has no undoer!

INCANTATION—CONSECRATING SPACE.
ali-ia (zab-ban) ali-ia (zab-ban)
My city is [Zabban]. My city is [Zabban].
šá ali-ia (zab-ban)-ta abullatimeš-šú-it
My city of [Zabban] has two Gates:
ana sit dšamši šá-ni-tu ana erib dšamši-it
The first is on the east, the second on the west.
[45] ana si-it dšamšiši šá-ni-tu ana e-rib dšamšiši
One is for the sunrise, one is for the sunset.
a-na-ku e-ra ha-as-ba šam-maštakal na-šá-ku
I am lifting to you my seed [*maskatal*].
a-na ilimeš šá šamêe mêmeš a-nam-din
To the Sky Gods I bring water.
kîma ana-ku ana ka-a-šú-nu ul-la-lu-ku-nu-ši
As do I come to purify you
at-tu-nu ia-a-ši ul-li-la-in-ni
so come forth to purify me!

INCANTATION—GRAND INVOCATION.

[50] ak-la ni-bi-ru ak-ta-li ka-a-ru

I have barred-up the river-crossing and harbor,

ak-li ip-ši-ši-na šá ka-li-ši-na ma-ta-a-ti

I hold back the magick of all lands;

A-NIM u AN-TUM iš-pu-ru-in-ni

ANU and ANTU have sent me here

man-nu lu-uš-pur a-na BE-LIT-sêri

but whom should I send to BELIT-SERI?

ana pî lúkaššapi-ia u kaššapti-ia i-di-i hur-gul-li

In the mouth of the evil warlock and witch, gag!

[55] i-di-i šipat-su šá apqal ilimeš MARDUK

By the incantation of the Magician God, MARDUK!

lil-sa-ki-ma la tap-pa-li-ši-na-a-ti

They will call upon you, but do not answer them;

liq-ba-nik-ki-ma la ta-šim-me-ši-na-a-ti

They will come before you, but do not listen to them.

lu-ul-si-ki-ma a-pu-ul-in-ni

Only should I call to you, should you answer me:

lu-qu-ba-ki-ma ši-min-ni ia-a-ti

Should I come before you, should you listen to me,

[60] ina qí-bit iq-bu-u A-NIM AN-TUM u BE-LIT-sêri

And to the covenant that ANU, ANTU and BELIT-SERI have issued!

MAQLU INCANTATION OF MARDUK.

šap-ra-ku al-lak '-ú-ra-ku a-dib-bu-ub

Where I am sent, I go. When ordered, I speak:

a-na li-it lúkaššapi-ia u kaššapti-ia ASAR-lú-du
BEL a-ši-pu-ti iš-pur-an-ni

Against the evil sorcerer and sorceress, *Aariluhi*
[MARDUK], Lord of the Incantation, has
sent me.

šá šamê qu-la šá irsitimtim ši-ma-a

Take note of what is in sky and on earth!

šá nâri qu-la-ni šá na-ba-li ši-ma-a amât-su

Take note of what is in the river and the word
spoken on land!

[65] šaru na-zi-qu tur-ru-uk e tal-lik

Wind, carrier of lightning, strike it down!

šá gišhatti u gišmar-te-e tur-ru-uk e tal-lak

The stick [image] is now broken, break it!

li-iz-zi-iz har-ra-an mârat ilimeš ra-butimeš

Let them stand waiting at the Gateway to the
Gods

a-di a-mat lúkaššapi-ia u kaššapti-ia a-qab-bu-ú

until I speak the Word to my evil sorcerer and
wicked witch.

šu'u i-pa-áš-šar immeru i-pa-áš-šar

The lamb will be freed! The sheep will be freed!

[70] a-mat-su-nu lip-pa-šir-ma a-ma-ti la ip-pa-
áš-šar

Their words may be loosened, but my Word
will not be.

a-mat a-qab-bu-ú a-mat-su-nu ana pân amâti-ia

lâ iparrik
**The Word that I speak, their words cannot
withstand it!**
ina qi-bit ASAR-lú-du BEL a-ši-pu-ti
**By the covenant of MARDUK, the Lord of the
Incantations!**

INCANTATION—CONSECRATION OF
IMAGES.

*[Images constructed are used in later
incantations.]*

NUSKU an-nu-tum salmânimeš e-piš-ia
NUSKU, these [images] are of my evil sorcerer.
an-nu-ti salmânimeš e-piš-ti-ia
These [images] are of my wicked sorceress;
[75] salmânimeš lúkaššapi-ia u kaššapti-ia
These [images] are of my warlock and witch,
salmânimeš e-piš-ia u muš-te-piš-ti-ia
These [images] are of my enchantress,
salmânimeš sa-hir-ia u sa-hir-ti-ia
These [images] are of my stupifier,
salmânimeš ra-hi-ia u ra-hi-ti-ia
These [images] are of my bewitchment,
salmânimeš BEL ik-ki-ia u BELIT ik-ki-ia
**These [images] are of my lord and lady
opponent,**
[80] salmânimeš BEL sir-ri-ia u BELIT sir-ri-ia
These [images] are of my lord and lady enemy.
salmânimeš BEL ri-di-ia u BELIT ri-di-ia

These [images] are of my lord and lady
  prosecutor.
salmânimeš BEL di-ni-ia u BELIT di-ni-ia
These [images] are of my lord and lady accuser.
salmânimeš BEL amâti-ia u BELIT amâti-ia
These [images] are of my lord and lady
  slanderer.
salmânimeš BEL daba-bi-ia u BELIT daba-bi-ia
These [images] are of my lord and lady
  defector.
[85] salmânimeš BEL egirri-ia u BELIT egirri-ia
These [images] are of my lord and lady nemesis.
salmânimeš BEL limutti-ia u BELIT limut-ti-ia
These [images] are of my lord and lady evil-
  doer.
*NUSKU da-a-a-nu tidu-šú-nu-ti-ma ana-ku la i-
du-šú-nu-ti*
NUSKU, only you know them. I do not know
  them,
šá kiš-pu ru-hu-u ru-su-u up-šá-še-e lim-nu-ti
their trick, their magick, their evil spells,
ip-šá bar-tum a-mat li-mut-ti râmu zêru
sorceries, manipulations, evil words, love, hate,
[90] dipalaa zitarrutâa kadibbidâa kúš-hunga
lying, murdering, confounding the truth of
  words,
šabalbalâa su-ud pa-ni ša-ni-e tè-mu
untrusting, quick to anger, lacking wisdom,
ma-la ibšu-u-ni is-hu-ru-ni u-šá-as-hi-ru-ni
everything that they have drawn to them,

an-nu-tum šú-nu an-nu-ti salmânimeš-šu-nu

these are those things; these are their [images],

kima šu-nu la iz-za-az-zu salmânimeš-šu-nu na-šá-ku

because the [images] cannot stand up, I lift
  them toward you,

*[95] at-ta NUSKU u ANU ka-šid lim-nu u a-a-bi
kušus-su-nu-ti-ma ana-ku la ah-hab-bil*

NUSKU and ANU, you who captures enemies,
  catch mine before I am destroyed!

*šá salmânimeš-ia ib-nu-u bu-un-na-an-ni-ia ú-
maš-ši-lu*

Those others that make my [images] and mimic
  my form,

pani-ia ú-sab-bi-tú kišâdi-ia ú-tar-ri-ru

they attack my face, they tie up my neck,

irti-ia id-i-bu esemti-ia ik-pu-pu

they hit my chest, they bend up my back.

a-hi-ia un-ni-šu ni-iš lib-bi-ia is-ba-tu

they make my arms weak and remove my
  strength,

*[100] lib-bi ilimeš itti-ia ú-za-an-nu-ú emûqi-ia
un-ni-šu*

they make the Spirit of the Lord angry with me
  and removed my strength,

li-it a-hi-ia iš-pu-ku bir-ki-ia ik-su-ú

they stripped the strength from my arms, and
  my knees are plagued with pain,

man-ga lu-'-tú ú-mal-lu-in-ni

they cause me to faint,

akâlemeš kaš-šá-pu-ti ú-šá-ki-lu-in-ni
they cause me to eat accursed food,
mêmeš kaš-šá-pu-ti iš-qu-in-ni
they cause me to drink foul water,
[105] rim-ki lu-'-ti ú-ra-me-ku-in-ni
they have purified me with unclean water,
nap-šal-ti šam-me lim-nu-ti ip-šu-šu-in-ni
they have washed me in juice of unclean seeds,
ana lúmiti i-hi-ru-in-ni
they have mocked me as though I am dead,
mêmeš napištimtim-ia ina qab-rì uš-ni-lu
they have placed my spirit among the dead,
ilu šarru BELU u rubû it-ti-ia ú-za-an-nu-ú
**they have made my god, king and master angry
with me;**
[110] at-ta GIRRA qa-mu-ú lúkaššapu u kaššaptu
**GIRRA [*Fires of God*] who burns the evil
   warlock and witch,**
mu-hal-liq rag-gi zêr lúkaššapi u kaš-šapti
**Who slays the evil offpsring of the warlock and
   witch,**
mu-ab-bit lim-nu-ti at-ta-ma
Who slays the evil-doers? It is You!
ana-ku al-si-ka ki-ma SAMAS u ANU
**I call upon you like SAMAS [*Shammash*] and
   ANU**
di-i-ni di-ni purussâ-ai purusus
Make me right, be the judge of my decision!
[115] qu-mu lúkaššapu u kaššaptu
Burn the evil sorcerer and sorceress!

a-kul ai-bi-ia a-ru-uh lim-nu-ti-ia
**Be the eater of my enemies, consume all those
who wish me evil!**
ûm-ka iz-zu lik-šu-šu-nu-ti
May they catch your roaring flames!
ki-ma mêmeš nâdi ina ti-qi liq-tu-ú
May their lives end like sewage!
*ki-ma ti-rik abnêmeš ubânâtimeš-šú-nu liq-ta-as-
si-sú*
**May their fingers be wrecked like those of
stone-masons, chewed off!**
[120] ina qi-bi-ti-ka sir-ti šá lâ innakaruru
By the name of the Glorious Command
ù an-ni-ka ki-nim šá lâ innennuú
and your Everlasting Covenant!

INCANTATION—CONSECRATION OF FIRE.

NUSKU šur-bu-ú i-lit-ti da-nim
NUSKU, Mighty Offspring of ANU
tam-šil abi bu-kur EN-LIL
**True [image] of your father, firstborn of
ENLIL,**
tar-bit apsî bi-nu-ut dBEL šamêe irsitim
**Son of the Abyss, Son of the Lord of
Heaven-Earth**
[125] áš-ši tipâra ú-nam-mir-ka ka-a-šá
I lift the torch and illuminate you,
lúkaššapu ik-šip-an-ni kiš-pi ik-šip-an-ni ki-šip-šú

The wicked sorcerer who has cursed me, curse
  him with the spell [he] used on me!
kassaptutak-šip-an-ni kiš-pi tak-šip-an-ni ki-šip-ši
The wicked witch who has cursed me, curse her
  with the spell [she] used on me!
e-pi-šu i-pu-šá-an-ni ip-šú i-pu-šá-an-ni e-pu-su
The sorcerer who has ensnared me, ensnare
  him with the spell [he] used on me!
e-piš-tu te-pu-šá-an-ni ip-šú te-pu-šá-an-ni e-pu-si
The sorceress who has ensnared me, ensnare
  her with the spell [she] used on me!
*[130] muš-te-piš-tu te-pu-šá-an-ni ip-šú te-pu-šá-
an-ni e-pu-si*
The enchantress who bewitched me; now
  bewitch her with the spell [she]
  used on me!
šá salmânimeš ana pi-i salmânimeš-ia ib-nu-ú
Who made [images] in my [image] and mim-
icked my shape;
*bu-un-na-an-ni-ia ú-mašši-lu ru'ti-ia il-qu-ú šârti-
ia im-lu-su*
they drained my saliva, they ripped at my hair,
sissikti-ia ib-tu-qu e-ti-qu epirhi.a šêpê-ia is-bu-su
they cut hems from my robe and steak the earth
  where my foot falls.
GIRRA qar-du šipat-su-nu li-pa-áš-šir
GIRRA [*Fires of God*], undo their incantation!

INCANTATION—OPENING RITE OF THE BURNINGS.

[135] anašiši ti-pa-ru salmânimeš-šú-nu a-qal-lu
I raise up the torch that I may burn the figures
šá ú-tuk-ku še-e-du ra-bi-su e-tim-mu
of the Demon, the Spirit, the Lurking Ghost,
la-maš-ti la-ba-si ah-ha-zu
the [lamastu], the [labasu], the [ahhazu],
lúlilu flilitu ardat lili
the [lilu], the [lilitu], the [nightmare],
ù mimma lim-nu mu-sab-bi-tu a-me-lu-ti
and any evil that plagues humanity:
[140] hu-la zu-ba u i-ta-at-tu-ka
dissolve, melt, drip away like wax!
qu-tur-ku-nu li-tel-li šamê
May your smoke drift ever upwards
la-'-mi-ku-nu li-bal-li dšamši
and may the Sun extinguish your coals!
lip-ru-us ha-a-a-ta-ku-nu mâr EA maš-mašu
May he extinguish your emenations,
   by the son of ENKI [who is MARDUK],
   Master of Magicians.

THE MAQLU SERIES – TABLET II

INCANTATION—USING A TALCUM IMAGE.

NUSKU šur-bu-ú ma-lik ilîmeš rabû-timeš
NUSKU, Mighty Counselor of the Great Gods!

pa-qid nindabêmeš šá ka-la IGIGI
Overseer of the sacrifices of all IGIGI,
mu-kin ma-ha-zi mu-ud-di-šu parakkêmeš
**Founder of cities, who reviews the Seats of
   Gods!**
u-mu nam-ru šá qi-bit-su si-rat
**Brilliant shining day, the promise of all
   goodness,**
[5] sukkal A-NIM še-mu-ú pi-ris-ti EN-LIL
**Messenger of ANU, obeying the secret of
   ENLIL,**
še-mu-ú EN-LIL ma-li-ku ša-du-ú IGIGI
Commander ENLIL, counselor of the IGIGI,
gaš-ru ta-ha-zu šá ti-bu-šú dan-nu
Powerful in combat, whose rising is powerful,
NUSKU a-ri-ru mu-šab-riq za-ai-ri
**NUSKU, brilliant shinning one who blinds his
   enemies,**
ina ba-li-ka ul iš-šak-kan nap-ta-na ina é-kur
without you there is no meal in the E.KUR,
*[10] ina ba-li-ka ilîmeš rabûtimeš ul is-si-nu qut-
rin-nu*
**without you, the Gods do not rise to smell the
   incense,**
ina ba-li-ka SAMAS u ANU ul i-da-a-ni di-i-nu
**without you, SAMAS and ANU do not hold
   court.**
*ha-sis šu-me-ka te-it-tir ina i-dir-ti ta-ga-mil ina
pušqi*
Whosoever remembers your name, you deliver

[him] from difficulty, sparing [his] miseries.

*ana-ku ardu-ka annanna apil annanna šá ilu-šú
annanna IŠTAR-šú annannitumtum*

**I am your servant __, son of __, whose god is __
and whose goddess is __.**

*as-hur-ka eš-e-ka na-šá-a qâtâ-ai šá-pal-ka ak-
mis*

**I turn to you, seek you out, hands raised; I
throw myself at your feet:**

[15] qu-mi kaš-šá-pi ù kaš-šap-ti

Burn the evil warlock and the wicked witch,

*šá lúkaššapi-ia u kaššapti-ia ár-hiš ha-an-tiš nap-
išta-šú-nu lib-li-ma*

**My warlock and witch, may they lose their life
quickly.**

*ia-a-ši bul-lit-an-ni-ma nar-bi-ka lu-šá-pi dà-li-li-
ka lud-lul*

**Spare my life so I will be forever in your debt,
alive to praise your greatness all my days!**

COUNTERSPELL—USING A SALT, COP-
PER OR TALCUM IMAGE.

GIRRA BELu git-ma-lu gaš-ra-a-ta na-bi šum-ka

**GIRRA, "You are powerful" is the meaning of
your name.**

[20] dnanna-ra-ta na-bi šum-ka

NANNA, your eyes see all things.

tuš-nam-mar bitatimeš ka-la-ma

Your light brightens dark places, light of the

moon over all countries.
tuš-nam-mar gi-im-ra ka-liš ma-ta-a-ti
**Your light brightens all things, so I stand before
   you,**
áš-šu at-ta ta-az-za-zu-ma
because you restore divine Justice.
ki-ma NANNA-SIN ù SAMAS ta-din-nu di-i-nu
**Like NANNA-SIN & SAMAS you make things
   right,**
[25] di-e-ni di-ni purussâ-a-a purusus
**So restore the right in my life, be a judge of my
   decision.**
a-na nûri-ka nam-ri az-ziz
To your brilliant shinning light, I come.
a-na elle-ti ti-pa-ri-ka az-ziz
To the brilliant shinning torch, I come.
BELU sissiktu-ka as-bat
Lord, I grab at the hem of your robe,
sissikat ilu-ti-ka rabi-ti as-bat
the hem of your divine robe I am grabbing.
[30] <unreadable part> -si il-ta-si eli-ia is-bat
lìb-bi qaqqadi kišâdi-ia u muh-hi
**[She] attacks the heart, the head, the neck and
   the face.**
is-bat ênê-ia na-ti-la-a-ti
[She] attacks my watchful eyes,
is-bat sêpê-ia al-la-ka-a-ti
attacks my walking feet,
is-bat bir-ki-ia ib-bi-ri-e-ti
attacks my moving knees [joints],

[35] is-bat idê-ia mut-tab-bil-a-ti
attacks my strengthened arms.
e-nin-na ina ma-har ilu-ti-ka rabîtiti
Now I come before your Divine Greatness,
salmânimeš siparri it-gu-ru-ti
[I set before you] the 'crossed' copper [images]
lúkaššapi-ia u kaššapti-ia
of my evil warlock and wicked witch,
e-piš-ia u muš-te-piš-ti-ia
my sorcerer and sorceress,
[40] sa-hir-ia u sa-hir-ti-ia
my stupifier and stupifyress,
ra-hi-ia u ra-hi-ti-ia
my enchanter and enchantress,
BEL ik-ki-ia u BELIT ik-ki-ia
my lord and lady who opposes me,
BEL sir-ri-ia u BELIT sir-ri-ia
my lord and lady who is my enemy,
BEL ri-di-ia u BELIT ri-di-ia
my lord and lady who prosecutes me,
[45] BEL di-ni-ia u BELIT di-ni-ia
my lord and lady who accuses me,
BEL amâti-ia u BELIT amâti-ia
my lord and lady who slanders against me,
BEL dabâbi-ia u BELIT dabâbi-ia
my lord and lady defector,
BEL egirri-ia u BELIT egirri-ia
my lord and lady nemesis,
BEL limuttimtim-ia u BELIT limuttimtim-ia
my lord and lady evil-doers:

[50] ana lúmiti pu-qu-du-in-ni
They gave me over to the dead;
nam-ra-su kul-lu-mu-in-ni
They bound me in their ridicule,
utukku lim-nu lu-u alû lim-nu lu-u etim-mu lim-nu
to the evil [*utukku*] or evil [*alu*] or [*etimmu*],
gallû lim-nu lu-u ilu lim-nu lu-u râbisu lim-nu
the evil [*gallu*] or evil god [*ilu*] or [*rabisu*],
lamaštu lu-u labasu lu-u ahhazu
the evil [*lamastu*] or [*labasu*] or [*ahhazu*]
[55] lúlilu lu-u flilitu lu-u ardat lili
the evil [*lilu*] or [*lilitu*] or [*ardat lili*]
lu-u li-'-bu si-bit šadi
or evil fever, like the [*sibit sadi*] disease,
lu-u be-en-nu ri-hu-ut dšul-pa-è-a
or befallen with epilepsy and seizures,
lu-u AN-TA-ŠUB-BA lu-u DINGIR-HUL
or [*antasubba*] or the "Evil God",
lu-u ŠU-DINGIR-RA lu-u ŠU-IN-NIN-NA
or "Hand of God" or "Hand of Goddess,"
[60] lu-u ŠU-GIDIM-MA lu-u ŠU-UDUG
**or "hand" of the Spirit of the Dead or of
[*utukki*]**
*lu-u ŠU-NAM-LÚ-LÍL-LU lu-u la-maš-tu sihirtutú
marat A-NIM*
**or "hand" of a human or [*lamastu*] Anu's
  daughter,**
lu-u SAG-HUL-HA-ZA mu-kil rêš li-muttim
or [*sagulaza*], the record-keeper of debts,
lu-u di-kis šêrêmeš šim-ma-tú ri-mu-tú

or the roasting of flesh, paralysis, consumption,
lu mimma lim-nu šá šu-ma la na-bu-u
or everything bad that is without names,
[65] lu mimma e-piš li-mut-ti šá a-me-lu-ti
or anything that is baneful to human beings,
šá sab-ta-ni-ma mu-ša u ur-ra iredú-nimeš-ni
that which makes me a prisoner at night, that
   which chases me during the day,
ú-hat-tu-ú šêrêmeš-ia kal u-mi sab-ta-ni-ma
that which eats my flesh, seizes my body,
kal mu-si la ú-maš-šar-an-ni
which will not give me rest for a single night!
e-nin-na ina ma-har ilu-ti-ka rabîtiti
Now, I come before your Divine Greatness,
[70] ina kibri-dit ellititi a-qal-li-šú-nu-ti a-šar-rap-šú-nu-ti
I burn and incinerate them completely with
   sulfur.
nap-li-sa-an-ni-ma be-lum ú-suh-šú-nu-ti ina zum-ri-ia
Look favorably on me, tear them out of my
   body,
pu-šur kiš-pi-šú-nu lim-nu-ti
disintegrate their evil spell!
at-ta GIRRA be-lum a-li-ki i-di-ia
GIRRA [*fires of God*] be at my side,
bul-lit-an-ni-ma nar-bi-ka lu-šá-pi dà-li-li-ka lud-lul
Keep me alive that I may praise, adore and
   serve.

COUNTERSPELL—USING A COPPER OR DOUGH & SULFUR IMAGE.

GIRRA a-ri-ru bu-kur A-NIM
GIRRA [*fires of God*] born of ANU,
da-'-in di-ni-ia at-me-e pi-ris-ti at-ta-ma
who guides my hearing and judges my decision;
ik-li-e-ti tu-uš-nam-mar
you bring the darkness to light,
e-šá-a-ti dal-ha-a-ti tu-uš-te-eš-šir
you bring order to the chaos or destroyed;
[80] a-na ilimeš rabûtimeš purussâa ta-nam-din
to the Great Gods you grant resolutions,
šá la ka-a-ta ilu ma-am-man purussâa ul i-par-ra-as
but for you no God makes your decisions.
at-ta-ma na-din ur-ti ù te-e-me
It is for you to give order and directions;
e-piš lum-ni at-ta-ma ar-hiš ta-kam-mu
you alone bind the evil and the evil-doer,
lim-nu ai-bu ta-kaš-šad ar-hiš
you strike down the evil enemy with swiftness.
[85] a-na-ku annanna mar ili-šu šá ilu-šú annanna IŠTAR-šu annannitum
I am __ , a son of his god, whose god is __ and whose goddess is __.
ina kiš-pi lu-up-pu-ta-ku-ma ma-har-ka az-ziz
I am bewitched, this is why I have come to you!
ina pân ili u šarri na-zu-ra-ku-ma du ana mah-ri-ka
Before God and King I have turned toward

you!

elî a-me-ri-ia mar-sa-ku-ma šá-pal-ka ak-mis

**Unpleasant to behold, I throw myself before
    you!**

GIRRA šur-bu-ú ilu el-lu

GIRRA – Radiant Fires of God!

[90] e-nin-na ina ma-har ilu-ti-ka rabîtiti

I come before your Divine Greatness,

*salmanimeš lúkaššapi u kaššapti šá siparri e-pu-
uš qa-tuk-ka*

**I have made two [images] of the evil warlock
    and wicked witch, in copper, by your hand:**

ma-har-ka ú-gir-šú-nu-ti-ma ka-a-šá ap-kid-ka

**In front of you I have 'crossed' them, I give
    them over to you.**

šu-nu li-mu-tu-ma ana-ku lu-ub-lut

Cause them death that I may live!

šu-nu li-ti-ib-bi-ru-ma ana-ku lu-ši-ir

Their paths detract, but I go straight!

[95] šu-nu liq-tu-ú-ma ana-ku lu-um-id

They reach limits, but I continue to grow!

šu-nu li-ni-šu-ma ana-ku lu-ud-nin

They become weak, but I continue to be strong!

GIRRA šar-hu si-ru šá ilimeš

GIRRA, brilliant flame among the gods,

*ka-šid lim-ni u ai-bi kušus-su-nu-ti-ma a-na-ku la
ah-hab-bil*

**you seize the evil and evil-doer; seize them so I
    may not be destroyed,**

ana-ku ardu-ka lul-ub-lut lu-uš-lim-ma ma-har-ka

lu-uz-ziz
**I, your servant, may remain living safe, able to
stand in front of you!**
[100] at-ta-ma ili-ia at-ta-ma be-li
You are my god, my lord supreme,
at-ta-ma da-ai-ni at-ta-ma ri-su-ú-a
You are my judge, my divine assistance,
at-ta-ma mu-tir-ru šá gi-mil-li-ia
You are my avenger, avenge me!

COUNTERSPELL—USING A COPPER OR BRONZE IMAGE.

GIRRA a-ri-ru mar da-nim qar-du
GIRRA [*fires of God*] raging fire born of ANU!
[105] iz-zu ahemeš-šú at-ta
Straightforward among your brethren;
*šá ki-ma NANNA-SIN u SAMAS ta-da-an-nu di-i-
nu*
**Like NANNA-SIN and SAMAS you make
things right.**
di-i-ni di-ni purussâ-ai purusus
Grant me justice, be the judge of my decision.
qu-mi kaš-šá-pi ù kaš-šap-ti
Burn the evil warlock and wicked witch!
GIRRA qu-mu lúkaššapi u kaššapti
GIRRA, burn the warlock and witch!
[110] GIRRA qu-li lúkaššapi u kaššapti
GIRRA, boil the warlock and witch!
GIRRA qu-mi-šú-nu-ti

GIRRA, incinerate them to nothing!
GIRRA qu-li-šú-nu-ti
GIRRA, boil them down!
GIRRA ku-šu-us-su-nu-ti
GIRRA, seize them!
GIRRA a-ru-uh-šú-nu-ti
GIRRA, devour them!
[115] GIRRA su-ta-bil-šú-nu-ti
GIRRA, remove them!
e-piš kiš-pi lim-nu-ti u ru-hi-e la tabûtimeš
They who inflict evil and the baneful spell,
šá a-na li-mut-ti ik-pu-du-ni ia-a-ši
Who think upon me with evil intention:
dan-nu ma-ak-kur-šu-nu šu-ul-qi
Let a criminal steal their possessions!
šu-bil bu-šá-šu-nu ik-ki-e-ma
Let a thief make off with their property!
[120] elî ma-na-ha-te-šu-nu hab-ba-ta šur-bi-is
Let a burglar invade their home!
GIRRA iz-zu git-ma-lu ra-šub-bu
GIRRA, wrathful, perfect and all-powerful
ina é-kur a-šar tal-lak-ti-ka tu-šap-šah-šu-nu-ti a-di sur-riš
In E.KUR, when you return, you will find peace!
ina a-mat E-A ba-ni-ka ù SAMAS an-nam-ru
By the incandation of ENKI, your progenitor and of SAMAS, I have become radiant;
apqallê šuut eri-du lik-pi-du-šú-nu-ti ana limnut-timtim

May the seven [*apkallu*] of ERIDU look onto
them with evil intention!

COUNTERSPELL—USING A CLAY IMAGE.

GIRRA gaš-ru u-mu na-an-du-ru
GIRRA, commanding force of terrible weather!
tuš-te-eš-šir ilimeš u ma-al-ki
You lead the gods and peoples rightfully!
ta-da-a-ni di-EN hab-li u ha-bil-ti
You lead the trials of the oppressed peoples;
ina di-ni-ia i-ziz-za-am-ma ki-ma SAMAS qu-ra-du
be also present at my trial! Like SAMAS,
[130] di-i-ni di-ni purussâ-ai purusus
lead my trial and be judge of my decision.
qu-mi kaš-ša-pi u kaš-šap-ti
Burn the evil warlock and wicked witch!
a-kul ai-bi-ia a-ru-uh lim-nu-ti-ia
Devour my enemies, those who wish me evil!
ûm-ka iz-zu lik-šu-us-su-nu-ti [SU.EN]
**May they be caught up in your terrible
weather!**

COUNTERSPELL—USING A BRONZE OR ASPHALT IMAGE.

[135] GIRRA šar-hu bu-kur da-nim
GIRRA [*raging fires of God*] born of ANU!
i-lit-ti ellitimtim šá-qu-tum dša-la-aš

Radiant ray of the Great [*salas*]!
šar-hu id-di-šu-u zik-ri ilimeš ka-ai-nu
**Divine, ever-renewing, constant, Word of the
  Gods,**
na-din nin-da-bi-e ana ilimeš IGIGI
**who distributes the offerings to the gods
  [*IGIGI*],**
*šá-kin na-mir-ti a-na A-NUN-NA-KI ilimeš rabû-
timeš*
**who gives radiance to the ANUNNAKI—the
  Great Gods!**
[140] iz-zu GIRRA muš-har-mit a-pi
Raging GIRRA, who destroys the pathway,
GIRRA al-la-lu-ú mu-ab-bit isemeš u ab-nemeš
GIRRA, strength to destroy wood and stone,
qa-mu-ú lim-nu-ti zêr lúkaššapi u kaš-šapti
**who burns the evil seed of the warlock and
  witch,**
mu-hal-liq rag-gi zêr lúkaššapi u kaš-šapti
**who incinerates the wicked seed of the warlock
  and witch!**
ina u-mi an-ni-i ina di-ni-ia i-ziz-za-am-ma
Come to my trial this day, come raging!
[145] e-piš bar-ti te-na-na-a ku-šu-ud lim-nu
Maker of submission, who seizes all that is evil!
*kima salmânimeš an-nu-ti i-hu-lu i-zu-bu u it-ta-
at-tu-ku*
**Like these figures drip away, melting and dis
  solving away,**
lúkaššapu u kassaptuli-hu-lu li-zu-bu u lit-ta-at-tu-

ku
**may the evil warlock and wicked witch drip
away, melt and dissolve.**

COUNTERSPELL—USING AN ASPHALT
OR SESAME-BUTTER IMAGE.

ki-e-eš li-bi-iš ki-di-eš
KES. LIBES. KIDES!
[150] a-ra-ab-bi-eš na-ad-ri-eš
ARABBES NADRES!
nâš ti-pa-a-ri ra-kib šá-a-ri
Who carries a torch and rides on the wind!
li-ru-un hu-un-ti-i
LIRUN HUNTI!
ka-sá-a-šu i-za-an-nun
KASAYASU IZANNUN!
ki-ma šá-ma-me el-ku-un
Rain down upon them from the heavens!
[155] ki-ma siri li-te-ru-ba-ma i-sá-a
Like a snake, bring them in, go hither!
*lik-tum-ku-nu-si siptu iz-zi-tú rabîtutú šá E-A
mašmaši*
**By the incantation of ENKI and [MARDUK]
    Master of Magicians,**
ù tu-kug-ga-e šá NIN-a-ha-qud-du
Rain down, you of NINAHAQUDDU,
li-la-ap-pit bu-un-na-an-ni-ku-nu
May they destroy the evil in existence!

COUNTERSPELL—USING A PLASTER
COVERED ASPHALT IMAGE.

[160] e-pu-šu-ni e-te-ni-ip-pu-šu-ni
They have performed magick (against me)!
ki-ma ki-i-ti ana ka-pa-li-ia
Like a ball of wool they have tried to roll me!
ki-ma hu-ha-ri ana sa-ha-pi-ia
Like a bird-clapper they have tried to catch me!
ki-ma ka-a-pi ana a-ba-ti-ia
**Like a mason stone they have tried to destroy
me!**
ki-ma še-e-ti ana ka-ta-me-ia
Like a net they have tried to ensnare me!
[165] ki-ma pi-til-ti ana pa-ta-li-ia
**Like a candlewick they have tried to snuff me
out!**
ki-ma pi-ti-iq-ti ana na-bal-ku-ti-ia
**Like a cliffwall they have tried to climb over
me!**
ki-ma mêmeš mu-sa-a-ti a-sur-ra-a ana mal-li-ia
With unclean waters they have tried to fill me!
ki-ma šu-šu-rat bîti ana bâbi ana na-sa-ki-ia
Like garbage they have tried to discard of me!
ana-ku ina qi-bit MARDUK u BEL nu-bat-ti
**I speak the incantation of MARDUK, Lord of
the Night**
[170] u ASARI-lú-du BEL a-ši-pu-ti
**and MARDUK [*asariludu*], the Master of
Magic[ians],**
e-pi-šu u e-piš-ti

the evil sorcerer and sorceress;
ki-ma ki-i-ti a-kap-pil-šu-nu-ti
like a ball of wool, I will roll them!
ki-ma hu-ha-ri a-sa-hap-šu-nu-ti
Like a bird-clapper, I take them down!
ki-ma ka-a-pi ab-ba-šu-nu-ti
Like a mason-stone, I destroy them!
[175] ki-ma še-e-ti a-kat-tam-šu-nu-ti
Like a net, I ensnare them!
ki-ma pi-til-ti a-pat-til-šu-nu-ti
Like a candlewick, I snuff them out!
ki-ma pi-ti-iq-ti ab-ba-lak-kit-šu-nu-ti
Like a cliff-wall, I climb over them!
ki-ma mêmeš mu-sa-a-ti a-sur-ra-a ú-ma-al-la-šú-nu-ti
With unclean waters I fill them up!
ki-ma šu-šu-rat bîti ana bâbi a-na-as-sik-šú-nu-ti
Like garbage, I discard them!
[180] titalliš lil-li-ka salam lúkaššapi u kaššapti
May the [image] of the evil warlock and wicked witch be burned to ash!

COUNTERSPELL—USING A TALCOM/SALT COVERED CLAY IMAGE.

at-ti man-nu kassaptuša ina nâri im-lu-'tita-ai
What is your name, witch? Who are you, who made an [image] of me from river-clay?
ina bîti e-ti-i ú-tam-me-ru salmanimeš-ia
Who burned my [image] in her dark house?

ina qab-rì it-mi-ru mu-ú-a
Who has spilled my water over a grave?
[185] ina tub-qí-na-ti ú-laq-qí-tu hu-sa-bi-e-a
Who has stolen sprigs of my fruit trees?
ina bit lúašlaki ib-tu-qu sissikti-ia
Who has cut seams of my robe?
ina askuppati iš-bu-šu epirhi.a šêpê-ia
Who has gathered up the earth beneath my feet?
áš-pur ana bâb ka-a-ri i-šá-mu-ú-ni li-pa-a-ki
I send to the harbor where you buy salt;
áš-pur ana hi-rit ali iq-ri-su-ú-ni ti-i-ta-ki
I send to the beach where you gather clay;
[190] áš-ta-pa-rak-kim-ma a-li-ku ti-nu-ru
I send you a furnace for your operations,
GIRRA mu-un-na-ah-zu
with GIRRA [fires of God] already lit,
GIRRA id-di-šu-u nur ilimeš ka-ai-nu
GIRRA [fires of God], constant light of the gods;
NANNA-SIN ina uruki SAMAS ina larsaki
NANNA-SIN in Ur, SAMAS in Larsa,
NERGAL a-di um-ma-na-ti-šú
NERGAL waiting next to his people,
[195] ISTAR a-ga-deki a-di ku-um-mi-šá
INANNA-ISHTAR in Akkad next to her house:
a-na la-qa-at zêri lúkaššapi u kaššapti
may they seize the seed of the evil warlock and wicked witch,
ma-la ba-šu-ú

no matter how numerous they may be,
kaššapta li-du-ku-ma ana-ku lu-ub-lut
may they kill the witch that I may remain alive!
áš-šu la e-pu-šá-áš-šim-ma i-pu-šá
I did not bewitch her, she bewitched me!
[200] áš-šu la as-hu-ra-áš-šim-ma is-hu-ra
I did not enchant her, she enchanted me!
ši-i tak-lat ana kiš-pi šá kit-pu-du-ú-ti
She believes in the spell she designed,
ù a-na-ku a-na ez-zu GIBIL da-a-a-nu
but I put my trust in GIBIL to be my judge!
GIRRA qu-mi-ši GIRRA qu-li-ši
GIRRA, burn [her], GIRRA incinerate [her]!
GIRRA šu-ta-bil-ši
GIRRA, strike [her] down!

COUNTERSPELL—USING A TALCUM DUSTED CLAY,
TAMARISK AND/OR CEDAR IMAGE.

at-ti man-nu kaššaptu šá tub-ta-na-in-ni
What is your name, witch? You who
  unceasingly pays me visits?
a-na li-mut-ti taš-te-ni-'-in-ni
Who looks for me with baneful intentions?
a-na la ta-ab-ti ta-as-sa-na-ah-hur-in-ni
Who looks for me with malicious intent?
al-ki ul i-di bit-ki ul i-di šum-ki ul i-di šu-bat-ki ul i-di
I don't know your city, your house or your

name.
[210] dšêdêmeš li-ba-'-ki
May the sedu [spirits] visit you,
utukkêmeš liš-te-'-u-ki
May the utukku [daemons] seek you out,
etimmêmeš lis-sah-ru-ú-ki
May the ghosts of the dead haunt you,
be-en-nu la ta-a-bu eli-ki lim-qut
May epilepsy seize you!
rabisêmeš li-mut-ti li-kil-lu rêš-ki
May the evil seat decapitate you!
<unreadable text>
GIBIL iz-zu la pa-du-u lìb-bi-ki lí-is-su-uh
GIBIL, furious, without pity, smite thee!
dgu-la a-zu-gal-la-tu rabitutu li-it-ki li-im-has
GULA, mighty physician, strike thee down!
GIBIL iz-zu zu-mur-ki li-ih-mut
GIBIL, furious, consume and burn your body!
[220] ellitumtum mârat da-nim šá šamê
Pure daughter of the Sky-God ANU,
šá ina kar-pat na-an-hu-za-at is-atu
who spreads herself in the Divine Vessel
libbi GIBIL qar-du sa-ma-a
bound with the hear of GIBIL, mighty hero...
<unreadable text>
[225] qu-mi ha-an-tiš šá lúkaššapi-ia u kaššapti-ia
incinerate quickly my evil warlock and wicked witch,
na-piš-ta-šú-nu lib-li-ma

uproot their existence!
ia-a-ši bul-lit-an-ni-ma nar-bi-ka lu-šá-pi
Allow me to live so that I may praise, honor and
dà-li-li-ka lud-lul
adore your name!

THE MAQLU SERIES – TABLET III

COUNTERSPELL—USING A CLAY OR WOODEN IMAGE.

[*You put the talcum on the stomach (of the image) and stuff the kidneys with wood.*]
kassaptu mut-tal-lik-tú šá sûqâ-timeš
The [witch] who (wanders) travels on the roads,
mu-tir-rib-tum šá bîtâtimeš
who invades the people's houses,
da-ai-li-tum šá bi-ri-e-ti
who walks in the alleyways,
sa-ai-di-tum šá ri-ba-a-ti
who hunts in the public district;
[5] *a-na pani-šá ù arki-šá is-sa-na-ah-hur*
she turns about, showing front and back,
izzazaz ina sûqi-ma ú-sah-har šêpê
she stays in place while still moving her feet,
i-na ri-bi-ti ip-ta-ra-as a-lak-tú
in the public district, she blocks the way.
šá etli damqi du-us-su i-kim
She steals the strength of the innocent man.
šá ardatu damiqtumtum i-ni-ib-šá it-bal

She steals the fruit of the innocent girl,
[10] i-na ni-kil-mi-šá ku-zu-ub-šá il-qi
and with one look, she takes away beauty,
etla ip-pa-lis-ma dûta-šu i-kim
she sees a man and takes his strength,
ardata ip-pa-lis-ma i-ni-ib-šá it-bal
she sees a girl and takes her beauty.
i-mu-ra-an-ni-ma kassaptuil-li-ka arki-ia
The witch saw me and followed,
i-na im-ti-šá ip-ta-ra-as a-lak-tú
and with her venom she has disrupted my way,
[15] i-na ru-hi-šá iš-di-hi ip-ru-us
with magick she has hindered my stride.
ú-šá-as-si ili-ia u ISTAR-ia ina zumri-ia
She takes me away from my god and my
  goddess.
šá kaššapti ina kul-la-ti aq-ta-ri-is tîta-šá
For the [image] of the witch I have used clay,
šá e-piš-ti-ia ab-ta-ni salam-šá
an [image] of the sorceress I have made.
áš-kun i-na lìb-bi-ki lipû ha-bil-ki
In your body I place [*talcum*], the destroyer
  of all.
[20] ú-sa-an-niš ina kalatimeš-ki e-ra qa-ma-ki
In your body I put wood to burn you with,
e-ra qa-ma-ki a-mat-ki lip-ru-us
the wood that burns and stops your venom!
e-li âli at-ta-pah i-šá-ti
Above the city, I kindle a fire;
ina šaplan âli at-ta-di lik-ti

beneath the city, I sprinkle a potion.
a-na bît ter-ru-ba at-ta-di i-šá-ti
Wherever you go, I set it on fire.
[25] te-pu-šim-ma GIBIL li-kul-ki
When you show yourself, GIBIL devours you!
tu-še-pi-šim-ma GIBIL lik-šu-ud-ki
When you rest yourself, GIBIL seizes you!
tak-pu-di-ma GIBIL li-duk-ki
When you move about, may GIBIL kill you!
tu-šak-pi-di-ma GIBIL lik-me-ki
When you breathe, may GIBIL burn you!
har-ra-an la ta-ri li-šá-as-bit-ki GIBIL ha-bil-ki
To the "Land of No Return" may GIBIL bring
you!
[30] GIBIL ez-zu zumur-ki li-ih-mut
GIBIL, raging force, burns your existence!

COUNTERSPELL—USING A TALCUM
IMAGE COVERED IN
REFUSE (GARBAGE).

-ta ši-na mârâtimeš da-nim šá šamêe
Two daughters of the Sky-God ANU,
ši-na mârâtimeš da-nim šá šamêe
Three daughters of the Sky-God ANU!
tur-ri ul-ta-nim-ma ul-tu šamêe ur-ra-da-ni
The descend from a ladder, from the sky!
e-ka-a-ma te-ba-ti-na e-ki-a-am tal-la-ka
When do you ascend? Where do you go?
[35] a-na e-pi-ši u e-piš-ti šá annanna apil an

nanna
The sorcerer and sorceress of ___ son of ___ ?
ana sahari ni-il-li-ka
We went to cast a spell,
a-na lu-uq-qu-ti šá hu-sa-bi-ši-na
We went to gather sprigs of their fruit-trees,
a-na hu-um-mu-mi šá hu-ma-ma-ti-ši-na
We went to gather up their garbage,
šá li-la-a-ti hu-lu-pa-qa a-na ša-ra-pi ni-il-li-ka
We went in the night to burn the *huluppu*-ship!

COUNTERSPELL—USING A WAX IMAGE.
[40] kassaptunir-ta-ni-tum
Sorceress. Murderess.
e-li-ni-tum nar-šin-da-tum
Nightmare. [*narsindatu*].
a-ši-ip-tum eš-še-pu-ti
[*aspitu*]. Priestess of the Magical Arts.
mušlahhatumtum a-gu-gi-il-tum
Snake-Charmer. [*agugiltu*].
qadištu naditu
Prostitute. [*naditu*].
[45] ISTAR-i-tum zêr-ma-ši-tum
ISHTAR-devotee, [*zermasitu*],
ba-ai-r-tum šá mu-ši
who captures the night,
sa-ayyu-di-tum šá kal u-mi
who hunts the whole of the day,
mu-la-'-i-tum šá šamêe

who putrefies the skies,
mu-lap-pit-tum šá irsitimtim
and touches down on earth,
[50] ka-mi-tum šá pî ilimeš
distorting the mouths of the gods,
ka-si-tum šá bir-ki ISTAR-âtimeš
binding up the knees of the goddesses,
da-ai-ik-tum šá etlêmeš
who kills the people's men,
la pa-di-tum šá dsin-nišâtimeš
who doesn't spare the women,
šá-ah-hu-ti-tum sab-bu-ri-tu
You are a destroyer – an evil woman!
[55] šá ana ip-ši-šá u ru-hi-šá la u-šar-ru man-ma
Against your sorceries and witchcraft none
   fight!
e-nin-na-ma e-tam-ru-ki is-sab-tu-ki
Now they see you – and they grab you,
uš-te-nu-ki uš-ta-bal-ki-tu-ki
they change you, they bring you to instability,
uš-ta-pi-lu a-mat ip-ši-ki
they have mixed up your magick word,
E-A u MARDUK id-di-nu-ki ana GIRRA qu-ra-di
ENKI and MARDUK; they cast you to GIRRA!
[60] GIRRA qu-ra-du ri-kis-ki li-ih-pi
GIRRA, may he burn your knots,
ù mimma ma-la te-pu-ši li-šam-hir-ki ka-a-ši
and every sorcery you spoke falls back on you!

COUNTERSPELL—USING AN ASPHALT IMAGE.

dit el-lu nam-ru qud-du-šu ana-ku
I am the Light! A pure river, shinning, I am!
e-pi-šu-u-a apqallu šá apsî
My sorcerer is the wise one of the deep.
e-pi-še-tu-ú-a mârâtimeš A-NIM šá šamêe
My sorceress are the daughters of ANU, the Sky-God.
[65] e-pu-šu-u-ni e-te-ni-ip-pu-šu-u-ni
They speak sorcery onto me unceasingly,
e-pu-šu-nim-ma ul ip-du-u zu-um-ri
they have bewitched and spared me nothing;
e-te-ni-pu-šu-nim-ma ul i-li-'-ú sa-ba-ti-ia
they endless work magick but cannot seize me!
a-na-ku e-pu-uš-ma pi-šu-nu as-bat
I have magick! And I catch their words in my hand!
e-te-bi-ib kima dit ina šadi-ia
I have become brilliantly shinning like the rivers in my land.
[70] e-te-lil ki-ma nam-ru ana bît purussî-ia
I have become pure as the Shinning One.
šá lúkaššapi-ia u kaššapti-ia
My evil warlock and wicked witch,
dit-ru na-bal-kat-ta-šú-nu lis-ku-nu-ma
the river, may it swallow them!
kiš-pu-šu-nu elî-šu-nu li-bal-ki-tu-ma
May their deceit come back on them,
a-na muh-hi-šu-nu u la-ni-šu-nu lil-li-ku

and fall upon them as dust on this [image]!
[75] ki-ma di-iq-me-en-ni li-is-li-mu pa-ni-šú-nu
May their burned face be blackened with ash!
li-hu-lu li-zu-bu u lit-ta-at-tu-ku
**May they drip [like wax], melt away and
dissolve,**
u ana-ku ki-ma dit ina šadî-ia lû ellêkuku
but I, like the river, remain pure!

COUNTERSPELL—USING AN ASPHALT
IMAGE NEXT TO A SULFUR IMAGE.

la-man-ni su-tu-ú e-la-mu-ú ri-da-an-ni
**The SUTI-tribesmen surround me; I am chased
by Elamites!**
kat-man-ni a-gu-ú e-du-ú sah-panan-ni
**I am surrounded by floodwater and raging
storms!**
[80] kassaptusu-ta-ta da-a-nu i-bit-su
The witch is of the SUTI-tribe, her attack fails!
e-le-ni-tu e-la-ma-ta li-pit-sa mu-ú-tu
**The nightmare is an Elamite whose hit means
death!**
GIBIL tap-pi-e SAMAS i-ziz-za-am-ma
GIBIL, friend of SAMAS, come forth unto me!
ki-ma šadi ina kibri-dit i-nu-uh-hu
Like the mountain comes to rest in sulfur,
kiš-pi ru-hi-e ru-si-e šá kaššapti-ia
**so may the sorceress and witches, the magick
spell of my evil-doers**

[85] e-li-ni-ti-ia GIBIL liq-mi
**and of my nightmares, may GIBIL burn them
all!**
dit ellu lib-ba-šá li-ih-pi
May the 'Pure River' break her heart!
mêmeš ellûtimeš lip-šu-ra kiš-pi-šá
May the 'Pure Water' dissolve her spell,
u ana-ku ki-ma dit ina šadî-ia lu ellêkuku
and I, like the river, remain pure!

COUNTERSPELL—USING A CLAY IMAGE
OR CYLINDER-SEAL.

[W*rite the "word"/name on a green cylinder-seal.*]
at-ti nam-nu kassaptušá bašûu
What is your name, witch?
[90] a-mat limuttimtim-ia ina lib-bi-šá
**In whose heart possesses the (evil spell) baneful
word,**
ina lišâni-šá ib-ba-nu-ú ru-hu-ú-a
**on whose tongue the (evil spell) baneful magic
forms,**
ina šap-ti-šá ib-ba-nu-ú ru-su-ú-a
on whose lips the spell against me starts?
i-na ki-bi-is tak-bu-us izzazaz mu-ú-tum
In your footsteps stands death.
kassaptuas-bat pi-ki as-bat lišân-ki
**Wicked Witch, I seize your words [tongue/
mouth],**
[95] as-bat ênê-ki na-ti-la-a-ti

I seize your eyes,
as-bat šêpê-ki al-la-ka-a-ti
I seize your feet,
as-bat bir-ki-ki e-bi-ri-e-ti
I seize your legs,
as-bat idê-ki mut-tab-bi-la-a-ti
I seize your right arm,
ak-ta-si i-di-ki a-na ar-ki-ki
then tie both arms behind your back!
[100] NANNA-SIN el-lam-mi-e li-qat-ta-a pagar-ki
May NANNA-SIN, twin-form, destroy your body,
a-na mi-qit mêmeš u išâti lid-di-ki-ma
cast you in a ditch of water of fire!
kassaptuki-ma si-hir kunukki an-ni-e
[Witch], like the interior of the furnace,
li-su-du li-ri-qu pa-nu-ú-ki
may your face become burnt yellow!

COUNTERSPELL—USING A CLAY IMAGE COVERED IN ASH & SOOT.
[Mix clumps of ash from a furnace and soot clinging to the pots with water and pour it over the head of your clay image.]
at-ti e šá te-pu-ši-in-ni [ISTAR--]
You have betwitched me [my goddess]!
[105] at-ti e šá tu-še-pi-ši-in-ni ...
You have charmed me!

at-ti e šá tu-kaš-ši-pi-in-ni
You have enchanted me!
at-ti e šá tu-hap-pi-pi-in-ni
You have oppressed me!
at-ti e šá tu-sab-bi-ti-in-ni
You have seized me!
at-ti e šá tu-kan-ni-ki-in-ni
You have suffocated me!
[110] at-ti e šá tu-ab-bi-ti-in-ni
You have destroyed me!
at-ti e šá tu-ub-bi-ri-in-ni
You have tied me!
at-ti e šá tu-ka-si-in-ni
You have bound me!
at-ti e šá tu-la-'-in-ni
You have confounded me!
tap-ru-si itti-ia ili-ia u ISTAR-ia
You have kept my God and Goddess from me,
[115] tap-ru-si itti-ia še-' še-tu ahu ahattu ib-ru
tap-pu u ki-na-at-tu
**kept away my friend, consort, brother, sister
  and family, companions and servants!**
*a-liq-qa-kim-ma ha-ha-a šá utuni um-mi-nu šá
diqâri*
**I scrape flakes of ash from the oven and soot
  from the pots,**
*a-mah-ha-ah a-tab-bak ana qaqqad rag-ga-ti šim-
ti-ki*
**I mix them with water and it drips over the
  head of your evil [image] figure.**

CONSECRATION—TWO IMAGES IN A CLAY BOAT IMAGE.

šá e-pu-šá-ni uš-te-pi-šá-an-ni

[She] Who has bewitched me? Who has enchanted me?

i-na mi-li nâri e-pu-šá-an-ni

In the river high waters, who has bewitched me?

[120] i-na mi-ti nari e-pu-šá-an-ni

In the river low waters, who has bewitched me?

a-na e-piš-ti ip-ši-ma iq-bu-ú

Who said to the sorceress, "Cast your sorcery"?

a-na sa-hir-ti suh-ri-ma iq-bu-ú

Who said to the inspired, "Make him insane"?

an-ni-tu lu-u maqurru-šá

This is her boat.

kima maqurru an-ni-tu ib-ba-lak-ki-tu

Like the boat crosses back across the waters,

[125] kis-pu-šá lib-bal-ki-tu-ma ina muh-hi-šá

so too may her spells come back and cross on her head

u la-ni-šá lil-li-ku

and her figure [body]! So be it!

di-in-šá lis-sa-hi-ip-ma di-e-ni li-šir

May [she] be defeated while I remain victorious!

COUNTERSPELL—USING TWO IMAGES
IN A CLAY BOAT.

[*Use the boat image with two figures inside.*]

maqurri-ia a-na NANNA-SIN ú-še-piš

My boat is built by NANNA-SIN,

ina bi-rit qârnemeš-šá na-šat pi-šir-tum

between the horns stands the potion as cargo;

[130] áš-bu ina lìb-bi-šá lúkaššapu u kaššaptu

inside it, the evil warlock and wicked witch sit;

áš-bu ina lìb-bi-šá e-piš u e-piš-tú

inside it, the sorcerer and sorceress sit;

áš-bu ina lib-bi-šá sa-hi-ru u sa-hir-tú

inside it, the inspirers of insanity sit.

šá maqurri-ši-na lib-ba-ti-iq a-šá-al-šá

Come, let the the dock-rope by cut!

mar-kas-sa-ši-na lip-pa-tir-ma tar-kul-la-šá

Come, let the moor be loosened from the boat!

[135] a-na qabal tam-ti liq-qil-pu LU ...

May it be lost in the midst of the sea!

e-du-u dan-nu a-na tam-tim li-še-si-šú-nu-ṭi

May a strong wave pull it into the ocean!

šam-ru-ti a-gu-u e-li-šú-nu li-tel-lu-u

May the waves of the sea overpower it!

šar-šú-nu a-a i-zi-qa-am-ma a-a i-hi-ta-a-ni

May a favorable wind not blow, not be had!

ina qi-bit NUSKU u GIRRA ilimeš dini-šú-nu

**By the order of NUSKU and GIRRA, the god-
  judges.**

COUNTERSPELL—USING A FLOUR-DOUGH IMAGE.

[140] LA-tú šá su-qa-ti am-me-ni tug-da-nar-ri-ÉN-ni

LATU, why do you pursue me in the street without ceasing?

am-me-ni na-áš-pa-tu-ki it-ta-na-lak-a-ni

Why send your messsages to my head?

kassaptu SAG.DUmeš a-ma-ti-ki

Witch, 'inhibited' is your new word!

-<unreadable text>

el-li a-na ú-ri ab-ta-ki a-<unreadable text>

I climb to the heights and see you!

[145] ú-rad a-na qaq-qa-ri-im-ma ú-sab-bi-tu

I climb down to earth and I see you!

ina kib-si-ki râbisa ú-še-šab

On your path, I set the BAN none may pass!

etim ri-da-a-ti harran-ki ú-šá-as-bit

On your path, I set the dead-spirit of persecution.

a-mah-ha-as muh-ha-ki ú-šá-an-na tè-en-ki

I strike at your head and confuse your mind,

a-dal-lah lìb-ba-ki ta-maš-ši-i šêrêmeš-ki

I bright your spirit to ruin, that you may forget your body,

[150] e-piš-tum u muš-te-piš-tum

sorcerer and sorceress of the deep!

šamûu a-na-ku ul tu-lap-pa-tin-ni

The sky, I am, and you cannot touch me.

irsitumtum a-na-ku ul tu-ra-hi-in-ni

The earth, I am, and you cannot confound me.
si-hi-il isbal-ti a-na-ku ul tu-kab-ba-si-in-ni
The thorn, I am, and you cannot crush me.
zi-qit aqrabi a-na-ku ul tu-lap-pa-tin-ni
**The scorpion's sting, I am, you cannot touch
me!**
[155] šadúu zaq-ru a-na-ku kiš-pi-ki ru-hi-ki
**The mountain peak, I am, and your sorceries
and enchantment,**
ru-su-ú-ki up-šá-šu-ki limnûtimeš
your spell, your evil manifestations,
la itehûmeš-ni la i-qar-ri-bu-u-ni ai-ši
cannot come close to me, you shall not pass!

CONSECRATION—USING A TALCUM IMAGE.

[The image is of a hand, made of talcum.]
rit-tu-ma rit-tu
Hand. Hand,
rit-tu dan-na-tu šá a-me-lu-ti
Hand, powerful of men,
[160] šá kîma nêši is-ba-tu a-me-lu
and like a lion, tackles the man,
kima hu-ha-ri is-hu-pu it-lu
**like a sling-shot, thrusts the man out to the
ground,**
kima še-e-ti ú-kat-ti-mu qar-ra-du
like a net, has ensnared the strong [man],
kima šu-uš-kal-li a-šá-rid-du i-bar-ru

like a grappling, has ensnared the leader,
kima giš-par-ri ik-tu-mu dan-na
**like a perfect trap, it has caught the most
powerful!**
*[165] lúkaššapu u kassapturit-ta-ku-nu GIRRA
liq-mi*
**The evil warlock and wicked witch, may
GIRRA burn your hands,**
GIRRA li-kul GIRRA liš-ti GIRRA liš-ta-bil
**GIRRA, devour. GIRRA, drink. GIRRA,
destroy!**
GIRRA lil-sa-a elî dan-na-ti rit-te-ku-nu
**GIRRA, scream out against [their] powerful
hands!**
šá rit-ta-ku-nu e-pu-šu zu-mur-ku-nu li-ih-mut
**Your hands are betwitched now, may [GIRRA]
burn the whole of your body now!**
li-is-pu-uh illat-ku-nu mâr E-A mašmašu
**May the son of ENKI, [MARDUK], Master of
the Magicians, destroy your power!**
[170] qut-ri GIRRA li-ri-ma pa-ni-ku-nu
Breath of GIRRA, blow against your face!
ki-ma ti-nu-ri ina hi-ta-ti-ku-nu
Like a furnace seeping through its defection,
ki-ma di-qa-ri ina lu-hu-um-me-ku-nu
Like a pot developing its soot,
li-is-pu-uh-ku-nu-ši GIRRA iz-zu
**May the raging GIRRA consume and destroy
you!**
ai ithumeš-ni kiš-pi-ku-nu ru-hi-ku-nu lim-nu-ti

**Your witchcraft, your evil spell, shall not come
  close to me!**
[175] e-til-la-a kima nûnêhi.a ina mêmeš-e-a
Climb like a fish in my own water,
kîma šahi ina ru-šum-ti-ia
Like a pig in my sty,
kîma šam-maštakal ina ú-sal-li
Like a seed [*mastakal*] from my meadows,
kîma šam-sassati ina a-hi a-tap-pi
Like the grass [reed] on the riverbanks,
kîma zêr isuši ina a-hi tam-tim
Like the seed of the black tree on the shore!
[180] el-lit ISTAR mu-nam-me-rat šim-ti
**Radiant shinning ISHTAR, who brightens the
  night,**
ú-su-rat balati us-su-ra-ku ana-ku
over to whose fate I have been delivered,
ina qi-bit iq-bu-ú GIRRA ra-šub-bu
**By the decree of the raging GIRRA [has
  spoken],**
ù GIRRA a-ri-ru mâr da-nim qar-du
and GIRRA the consuming, born of ANU

COUNTERSPELL—BURNING THE
TALCUM IMAGE.

[*Use the image of a hand made of talcum.*]
rit-tum-ma rit-tum
Hand. Hand,
[185] rit-tum dan-na-tum šá a-me-lu-ti

Hand, powerful of men,
kassaptuáš-šú pi-i-ki da-ab-bi-bu
Witch, because of your strong slander [mouth]
áš-šú dan-na-ti rit-ta-ki
because of your powerful [hand],
álu a-ma-tum áš-šak-ki
I have brought you the Word from the city,
bitu a-ma-tum ú-ba-a-ki
from the [secret] house, I seek the [secret] Word for you.
[190] lúkaššapu u kassaptue-piš u e-piš-tú
Evil warlock and wicked witch; sorcerer and sorceress,
bi-il rit-ta-ku-nu-ma ana išâti lud-di
I pull down your lifted hand and cast it into the fire!

THE MAQLU SERIES – TABLET IV

BANISHING RITUAL—USING TWO FIGURES & A REED CROSS.

[*Two reed pipes are filled with blood and excrement, lay them in a cross pattern in the middle of your circle. Make two figures of talcum and two figures of wax. Place these at the four points of the cross.*]
biš-li biš-li qi-di-e qi-di-e
Boil, boil, burn, burn!
rag-gu u si-e-nu e te-ru-ub at-lak

Discord and evil, do not enter, keep away!

at-ta man-nu mâr man-ni at-ti man-nu mârat man-ni

Who are you? Born of who? Whose son? Whose daughter?

šá áš-ba-tu-nu-ma ip-še-ku-nu up-šá-še-ku-nu

You who sit [t]here and plot your sorcery

[5] te-te-ni-ip-pu-šá-ni ia-a-ši

against me!

lip-šur E-A mašmašu

May ENKI the Magician

lis-bal-kit kiš-pi-ku-nu

undo and reverse your spells!

ASARI-lú-du mašmaš ilimeš mâr E-A apqallu

MARDUK [asariludu], Magician of the Gods, son of ENKI, wise father!

a-kas-si-ku-nu-ši a-kam-mi-ku-nu-ši a-nam-din-ku-nu-ši

I bind you! I tie you up! I give you over

[10] a-na GIRRA qa-mi-e qa-li-i ka-si-i

to GIRRA, burning, incinerating, consuming,

ka-ši-du šá kaššapâtimeš

overpowering and seizing the sorcer[ess]!

GIRRA qa-mu-ú li-tal-lal i-da-ai

GIRRA, incinerating power, give strength to my arms!

ip-šú bar-tu a-mat limuttim râmu zêru

Magick. Revolt. Baneful. Love. Hate.

dipalâa zitarrutâa kadibbidâ KUŠ.HUNGA

Chaos. Murder. Deceit [disease of the mouth].

[15] šabalbalâa su-ud pa-ni u šá-ni-e tè-e-mu
Tearing from the insides. A face turned to insanity.

te-pu-šá-ni tu-še-pi-šá-ni GIRRA lip-šur
What you have done, what you have made others do for you, may GIRRA reverse it!

a-na lúpagri ta-hi-ra-in-ni te-pu-šá-ni tu-še-pi-šá-ni GIRRA lip-šur
You have marked me for dead, may GIRRA undo this!

a-na gul-gul-la-ti tap-qí-da-in-ni te-pu-šá-ni tu-še-pi-šá-ni GIRRA lipšur
You have turned me over to the dead, may GIRRA undo this!

a-na etim kim-ti-ia tap-qí-da-in-ni te-pu-šá-ni tu-še-pi-šá-ni GIRRA lipšur
You have delivered me to the spirits of the dead, may GIRRA undo this!

[20] a-na etim a-hi-i tap-qí-da-in-ni te-pu-šá-ni tu-še-pi-šá-ni GIRRA lip-šur
You have delivered me to the spirits of the unknown dead, may GIRRA undo this!

a-na etimmi mur-tappi-du šá pa-qí-da la i-šu-u te-pu-šá-ni
*   tu-še-pi-šá-ni-GIRRA lip-šur*
You have given me to a wandering spirit, may GIRRA undo this!

a-na etim har-bi na-du-ti tap-qí-da-in-ni te-pu-šá-ni tu-še-pi-šá-ni-GIRRA lip-šur
You have turned me over to the ghost of ruins,

may GIRRA undo this!

a-na sêri ki-di u na-me-e tap-qí-da-in-ni te-pu-šá-ni tu-še-pi-šá-ni-GIRRA lip-šur

You have sent me into open desert to rot, may GIRRA undo this!

a-na dûri ù sa-me-ti tap-qí-da-in-ni te-pu-šá-ni tu-še-pi-šá-ni GIRRA lip-šur

You have pressed me up against the [inner and outer] walls, may GIRRA undo this!

[25] a-na dbe-lit sêri u ba-ma-a-ti tap-qí-da-in-ni te-pu-šá-ni tu-še-pi-šáni-GIRRA lip-šur

You have turned me over to the Mistress of the Mountains, may GIRRA undo this!

a-na utûn la-ab-ti tinûri kinûni KI.UT.BA ù nap-pa-ha-ti tap-qí-da-in-ni-te-pu-šá-ni tu-še-pi-šá-ni GIRRA lip-šur

You have delivered me into a furnace, on the stove-top, into pails of hot embers and coals, may GIRRA undo this!

salmânimeš-ia a-na lúpagri tap-qí-da te-pu-šá-ni tu-še-pi-šá-ni GIRRA lip-šur

You have given [images] of me to the dead, may GIRRA undo this!

salmânimeš-ia a-na lúpagri ta-hi-ra te-pu-šá-ni tu-še-pi-šá-ni GIRRA lip-šur

You have made [images] of me among the dead, may GIRRA undo this!

salmânimeš-ia it-ti lúpagri tuš-ni-il-la te-pu-šá-ni tu-še-pi-šá-ni GIRRA lip-šur

You have placed [images] of me next to the

dead, may GIRRA undo this!

[30] salmânimeš-ia ina sûn lúpagri tuš-ni-il-la te-
pu-šá-ni tu-še-pi-šá-ni-GIRRA lip-šur

You have placed [images] of me into the hands
  of the dead, may GIRRA undo this!

salmânimeš-ia ina qimah lúpagri taq-bi-ra te-pu-
šá-ni tu-še-pi-šá-ni-GIRRA lip-šur

You have buried [images] of me in the grave of
  the dead, may GIRRA undo this!

salmânimeš-ia a-na gul-gul-la-ti tap-qí-da te-pu-
šá-ni tu-še-pi-šá-ni-GIRRA lip-šur

You have turned [images] of me over to the
  dead, may GIRRA undo this!

salmânimeš-ia ina igâri tap-ha-a te-pu-šá-ni tu-
še-pi-šá-ni GIRRA lipšur

You have locked away [images] of me in the
  wall-safe, may GIRRA undo this!

salmânimeš-ia ina asquppati tuš-ni-il-la te-pu-šá-
ni tu-še-pi-šá-ni-GIRRA lip-šur

You have placed [images] of me at the baneful
  threshold, may GIRRA undo this!

[35] salmânimeš-ia ina bi-' šá dûri tap-ha-a te-pu-
šá-ni tu-še-pi-šá-ni-GIRRA lip-šur

You have locked up [images] of me at the
  baneful entrance, may GIRRA undo this!

salmânimeš-ia ina ti-tur-ri taq-bi-ra-ma um-ma-
nu ú-kab-bí-su te-pu-šáni tu-še-pi-šá-ni GIRRA
lip-šur

You have embedded [images] of me on a bridge,
  causing others to step on me, may GIRRA

undo this!

*salmânimeš-ia ina bu-ri iqi šá lúašlaki bûra tap-
ta-a taq-bi-ra te-pu-šá-ni-tu-še-pi-šá-ni GIRRA
lip-šur*

**You have embedded [images] of me in the wash-
house drains, may GIRRA undo this!**

*salmânimeš-ia ina iqi šá lúlâkuribbi bûra tap-ta-a
taq-bi-ra te-pu-šá-ni-tu-še-pi-šá-ni GIRRA lip-šur*

**You have buried [images] of me in the
gardener's [ditch], may GIRRA undo this!**

*salmânimeš-ia lu-u šá isbîni lu-u šá iserini lu-u šá
lipî*

**[You have made] ...images of me from wood and
salt,**

[40] lu-u šá ISKUR lu-u šá kuspi

from wax, from seed,

lu-u šá itti lu-u šá titi lu-u šá liši

from asphalt, from clay, from dough;

*salmânimeš sir-ri-ia pa-ni-ia u la-ni-ia te-pu-šá-
ma*

**images, likenesses of my face and form you
mold**

kalba tu-šá-ki-la šahâ tu-šá-ki-la

then give to a dog and a pig to eat,

issuru tu-šá-ki-la ana nâri taddâa

**given to the birds of the sky who drop them in
the river;**

[45] salmânimeš-ia a-na la-maš-ti mârat da-nim

**[given]...images of me to LAMASTU, daughter
of ANU,**

tap-qí-da te-pu-šá-ni tu-še-pi-šá-ni GIRRA lip-šur

**what you have given to do, what others have
done for you, may GIRRA undo this!**

*salmânimeš-ia a-na GIRRA tap-qí-da te-pu-šá-ni
tu-še-pi-šá-ni GIRRA lip-šur*

**...images of me given to GIRRA, you have done
this, may GIRRA undo this!**

*mêmeš-ia it-ti lúpagri tuš-ni-il-la te-pu-šá-ni tu-
še-pi-šá-ni GIRRA lipšur*

**You have poured my [water] in with the dead,
may GIRRA undo this!**

*mêmeš-ia ina sûn lúpagri tuš-ni-il-la te-pu-šá-ni
tu-še-pi-šá-ni GIRRA lip-šur*

**You have poured my [water] in the lap of the
dead, may GIRRA undo this!**

*[50] mêmeš-ia ina qimah l;úpagri taq-bi-ra te-pu-
šá-ni tu-še-pi-šá-ni-GIRRA lip-šur*

**You have poured my [water] into the grave of
the dead, may GIRRA undo this!**

*ina-tim mêmeš-ia taq-bi-ra te-pu-šá-ni tu-še-pi-šá-
ni GIRRA lip-šur*

**You have poured my [water] in the body of the
dead, may GIRRA undo this!**

*ina-tim mêmeš-ia taq-bi-ra te-pu-šá-ni tu-še-pi-šá-
ni GIRRA lip-šur*

**You have poured my [water] in the body of the
dead, may GIRRA undo this!**

*ina-me mêmeš-ia tah-ba-a te-pu-šá-ni tu-še-pi-šá-
ni GIRRA lip-šur*

You have siphoned the [water] from my body,

may GIRRA undo this!

mêmeš-ia ana Gilgameš ta-ad-di-na te-pu-šá-ni
tu-še-pi-šá-ni GIRRA lip-šur

To GILGAMESH you gave my water, may
GIRRA undo this!

[55] <unreadable text> li-e ta-hi-ra-in-ni te-pu-
šá-ni tu-še-pi-šá-ni-GIRRA lip-šur

You have lost my waters to the ditch, may
GIRRA undo this!

zikurudâa a-na pa-ni NANNA-SIN te-pu-šá-ni tu-
še-pi-šá-ni GIRRA lip-šur

You have slit my throat before NANNA-SIN,
may GIRRA undo this!

zikurudâa a-na pa-ni d-šul-pa-è-a te-pu-šá-ni tu-
še-pi-šá-ni GIRRA lipšur

You have slit my throat before SHUL-PA-EA,
may GIRRA undo this!

zikurudâa a-na pa-ni MULU-KA-DU-A

You have slit my throat in the starlight of
CYGNUS and LACERTA,

zikurudâa <unreadable text> te-pu-šá-ni tu-še-pi-
šá-ni GIRRA lip-šur

You have slit my throat... may GIRRA undo
this!

<unreadable text>

ina pân -zi u bâb bîti ma-

In front of the entrance gate of the house,

[65] ina pân ib-ri tap-pi u ki-na-at-ti KI.MINA

In front of friends, companions and servants [of
the house],

122

ina pân abi u ummi ahi u ahati mâri u mârti
KI.MINA
In front of parents and siblings [of the house],
ina pân bîti u bâbi ardi u amti sih-ri u ra-bi šá bîti
KI.MINA
In front of the house and gate, servants, both
small and large [of the house],
elî a-me-ri-ia tu-šam-ri-si-in-ni ...
You made me ugly to all those who behold me.
ak-ta-mi-ku-nu-ši ak-ta-si-ku-nu-ši at-ta-din-ku-
nu-ši
I have bound you, tied you up and delivered
you over
[70] ana GIRRA qa-mi-i qa-li-i ka-si-i
to GIRRA, who burns, incinerates, binds up
ka-ši-du šá kaššapâtimeš
and seizes the sorceress.
GIRRA qa-mu-ú li-pat-tir rik-si-ku-nu
GIRRA, burn away your knots, undo your
li-pa-áš-šir kiš-pi-ku-nu li-na-as si-ir-qi-ku-nu
enchantments and untie your ropes,
ina qí-bit MARDUK mâr E-A apqalli
by the decree of MARDUK, son of ENKI, the
Wise Father of Magicians,
[75] u GIRRA a-ri-ru ap-qal mâr da-nim qar-du
and GIRRA, praised and wise – born of ANU!

COUNTERSPELL—USING A WOODEN IMAGE.

[*Make an image using three branches of wood.*]
at-ti man-nu kassaptušá zitarrutâa êpušaša
Who are you, (whoever you are) sorcer[ess]?
Who has committed the murder?
lu-u ib-ru lu-u tap-pu-u
Whether companion or neighbor,
lu-u ahu lu-u it-ba-ru
whether family or friend,
lu-u ú-ba-ra lu-u mâr âli
whether foreigner or native,
[80] lu-u mu-du-u lu-u la mûdû
whether known or unknown
lu-u lúkaššapu lu-u kaššaptu
whether sorcerer or sorceress,
lu-u zikaru lu-u sinništu lu-ú hab-lu lu-ú ha-bil-ti
whether man or woman, murderer or murderess,
lu-u lúkur-gar-ru-u lu-u sah-hi-ru
whether *kugarru*-priest or *sahhiru*-priestess,
lu-u ... lu-u nar-šin-du-u lu-u muš-lahhêe
whether... or a *narsindu* or snake-charmer,
[85] lu-u a-gu-gi-lu-u lišanu nukur-tum šá ina mâti ibašši
whether an *agugilu* or an foreign traveller...

CONSECRATION—PREPARING IMAGES.

[105] i-pu-šá-ni i-te-ni-ip-pu-šá-ni
It hexes. It vexes, unceasingly.
gu-ti-e-ti e-la-ma-a-ti
The CUTHITES, the ELAMITES,
ma-rat ha-ni-gal-bat-a-ti
the daughters of the *hanigalbatians*,
6 ina mâti i-rak-ka-sa-a-ni rik-si
the six on dry earth bind knots,
6 riksi-ši-na 7 pit-ru-ú-a
six are their knots, seven is my untying.
[110] šá mûša ip-pu-sa-nim-ma
What they tie in the night,
šá kal u-mu a-pa-áš-šar-ši-na-ti
I untie in the day.
šá kal u-mu ip-pu-šá-nim-ma
What they tie in daylight,
šá mûša a-pa-áš-šar-ši-na-ti
I untie in the nighttime.
a-šak-kan-ši-na-a-ti ana pi-i GIRRA qa-mi-i
I turn them over to the burning, GIRRA,
[115] qa-li-i ka-si-i ka-ši-du
incinerating, binding and seizing
šá kaššapatimeš
the sorcer[esses]!

**MAQLU INCANTATION—BURNING THE
IMAGES.**
ru-'ú-a kaš-šá-pat ana-ku pa-ši-ra-ak

My anathema is a witch! I am released!
kassaptukas-šá-pat ana-ku pa-ši-ra-ak
The witch is a wicked witch, I am released!
kassaptu e-la-ma-a-ti ana-ku pa-ši-ra-ak
The witch is an ELAMITE, I am released!
[120] kassaptu qu-ta-a-ti ana-ku pa-ši-ra-ak
The witch is a CUTHITE, I am released!
kassaptu su-ta-a-ti ana-ku pa-ši-ra-ak
The witch is of the SUTI-tribes, I am released!
kassaptu lul-lu-ba-a-ti ana-ku pa-ši-ra-ak
The witch is a *lulluban*, I am released!
kassaptu ha-bi-gal-ba-at ana-ku pa-ši-ra-ak
The witch is a *hanigalbatan*, I am released!
kassaptu a-gu-gi-lat ana-ku pa-ši-ra-ak
The witch is an *agugiltu*, I am released!
[125] kassaptu nar-šin-da-at ana-ku pa-ši-ra-ak
The witch is an *narsindatu*, I am released!
kassaptu mušlahhat ana-ku pa-ši-ra-ak
The witch is a snake-charmer, I am released!
kassaptueš-še-ba-a-ti ana-ku pa-ši-ra-ak
The witch is a priestess of magick, I am
   released!
kassaptuqur-qur-ra-a-ti ana-ku pa-ši-ra-ak
The witch is a metallurgist, I am released!
kassaptuši-i râbis bâbi-ia ana-ku pa-ši-ra-ak
The witch is a spoke on my gate, I am released!
[130] kassaptumârat âli-ia ana-ku pa-ši-ra-ak
The witch is a neighbor of mine, I am released!
áš-pur a-na e-rib šamši salmânimeš-si-na il-qu-tu-ú-ni

I have gathered her [images] and sent them to the west.

šá u kaššapâtimeš salmânimeš-ši-na

The figures of the seven and the seven witches

ana GIRRA ap-qid

to GIRRA, I deliver.

ana ú-tu-ni a-lik-ti a-šar-rap-ši-na-ti

In a portable kiln I have burned them.

[135] GIBIL qu-mi lúkaššapi u kaššapti

GIBIL, burn the evil warlock and wicked witch!

GIBIL qu-li lúkaššapi u kaššapti

GIBIL, incinerate my warlock and witch!

GIBIL qu-mi-ši-na-a-ti

GIBIL, burn them completely!

GIBIL qu-li-ši-na-a-ti

GIBIL, incinerate them completely!

GIBIL kušus-si-na-a-ti

GIBIL, seize the whole of their being!

[140] GIBIL a-ru-uh-ši-na-a-ti

GIBIL, devour them completely!

GIBIL šu-ta-bil-si-na-a-ti

GIBIL, remove them away from here!

ez-zu GIBIL li-ni-ih-ka-na-ši

Roaring GIBIL, please calm down!

GIBIL lu-li-mu... li-ki-na-ši

GIBIL, [save me and] calm yourself!

lúkaššapu u kassaptue-piš u e-piš-tum

The sorcerer and sorceress, the enchanter and enchantress,

[145] šu-nu lu-u ...-kam-ma

may they truly [burn out completely]!

ana-ku mêmeš mîli-ma

though I let loose the floodwater

lu-u-ba-'-ši-na-a-ti

to shower down upon them!

THE MAQLU SERIES – TABLET V

BANISHING—USING A THYME & SESAME IMAGE.

e-piš-ti ù muš-te-piš-ti

My enchanter and my enchantress

áš-bat ina silli a-ma-ri ša libitti

sit in the shade of a stoop made of clay bricks.

áš-bat-ma ip-ši-ia ip-pu-šá i-ban-na-a salmânimeš-ia

[She] sits doing tricks, fashioning [images] of me.

a-šap-pa-rak-kim-ma šamhašutu u SAMAS-šammu

I send you thyme and sesame [literally 'sun-flower'].

[5] ú-sap-pa-ah kiš-pi-ki ú-tar amâtimeš-ki ana pî-ki

Your sorcery is anathema to me, your words fall back into your mouth!

ip-ši te-pu-ši lu-u šá at-tu-ki

The tricks you "turn" now turn against you!

salmânimeš tab-ni-i lu-u šá tè-me-ki

The [images] you made of me, may they now
  resemble you!
mêmeš tah-bi-i lu-u šá ra-ma-ni-ki
The waters [of mine] you siphoned are your
  own!
ši-pat-ki ai iq-ri-ba amâtmeš-ki ai ik-šu-da-in-ni
Your magick spell does not come close to me,
  your Word cannot reach where I [stand]!
*[10] ina qi-bit E-A SAMAS u MARDUK u rubâti
BELIT ilê*
By the incantation of ENKI, SHAMMASH and
  MARDUK [and among them] the Great Lady
  of the Gods [BELIT]!

INCANTATION—RITE OF PROTECTION.
man-nu pû ip-til utteta ú-qas-sir
Who has tried to [commit the unthinkable]?
ana šamêe kiš-pi ana irsitimtim bar-ta êpušuš
Who has ever bewitched Heaven or performed
magick against the Earth?
ana šamirri ilimeš rabûtimeš ip-šá bar-ta
Against the IRRI [*erra, NERGAL*], the Great
  Gods, who has ever cast magick [upon these],
amât limuttimtim man-nu ú-qar-rib
or spoken evil words against them?
[15] ki-ma pû la ip-pat-til uttatu la uk-ta-as-sa-ru
Just as the unthinkable cannot be done, neither
  can
ana šamêe kiš-pi ana irsitimtim bar-tu la in-ni-ip-

pu-šú
magick be done against Heaven or Earth.
ana mârat ilimeš rabûtimeš
[And so as] the daughter of the Great Gods;
ip-šá bar-tum amat limuttimtim lâ itehu lâ i-qar-ru-bu
magick, sorcery, baneful spells do not come close;
ip-šá bar-tum amât limuttimtim lâ iteha
[so too should] magick, sorcery, baneful spells not
[20] lâ i-qar-ru-ba ia-a-ši
come close to me!

INCANTATION—INVOCATION TO THE GODS.

[Make libations of water and altar offerings.]
u-un-na-nu du-un-na-nu pârisis pu-ru-us-si-e-ni
The UNNANU [ANUNNA], you who is fated our decisions,
i-na ma-har NUSKU u GIRRA šu-bil-te šak-na-at
In front of NUSKU and GIRRA my [image] is placed.
al-ki na-bal-kàt-tum šu-um-ri na-bal-kàt-tum
Come forth and attack! Rage on! Avenge me! Attack!
i-na na-sa-ah šêpê šá lúkaššapi-ia
When you tear off the feet of my sorcerer
[25] u kaššapti-ia šêpê-ki šuk-ni

130

and my sorceress, stamp your own feet down.
lillu li-bi-il-ma kassaptuana da-ai-ni-šá
**May the sorcer[ess] be dragged before the
   Judge!**
daianu-šá kîma nêši li-sa-a elî-šá
May [her] judge roar like a lion [at her]!
lim-has lêt-sa li-tir amât-sa ana pî-šá
**May he strike her face and cause her words to
   turn back into her mouth!**
e-piš-ti ù muš-te-piš-ti
Of the sorceress and 'greater' sorceress,
[30] ki-ma šamnini li-nu-šú kiš-pu-šá
Like mint, may her magick sting her!
ki-ma šamazupiri li-sap-pi-ru-ši kiš-pu-šá
Like saffron, may her magick scratch at her!
ki-ma šamsahli li-is-hu-lu-ši kiš-pu-šá
Like mustard, may her magick penetrate her!
ki-ma šam-KUR.ZI.SAR li-sa-am-mu-si kiš-pu-šá
**Like the weed [kurzisar], may her magick bind
   her up!**
ki-ma šamkasi li-ik-su-ši kiš-pu-šá
Like cassia, may her magick tie [them] up!
[35] ki-ma šamhašûti li-haš-šu-ši kiš-pu-šá
Like thyme, may her magick bind them up!
ki-ma kit-mi li-ik-tu-mu-ši kiš-pu-šá
Like alum, may her magick cover them up!
ki-ma šamirri li-ru-ru-ši kiš-pu-šá
**Like pumpkin-vine, may her magick strangle
   them up!**
ki-ma šamnuhurti lit-tah-hi-ra šapâtimeš-šá

Like *asafoetida*, may [their] lips swell up!
e-piš-ti ù muš-te-piš-ti
Of the sorceress and the 'greater' sorceress,
[40] lib-bal-kit-si sûqu ù su-lu-ú
**may the street and pathway give out around
them!**
lib-bal-kit-si ib-ra-tum ù ni-me-di-šá
May the room and chair give out beneath them!
lib-bal-ki-tu-ši-ma ilimeš šá sêri u âli
**May the God of the desert and city fall upon
them!**
*kassaptukima kalbi ina hatti kima an-du-hal-lat
ina kir-ban-ni*
**May someone chase the sorceress about like a
dog with a stick or like a serpent on the earth.**
*ki-ma kib-si immeri li-sa-am-me-ku-ši-ma li-ti-qu-
ši*
**[like a] chase through a sheep-path, pass over
them!**
*[45] ki-ma qur-sin-ni imêri ina sûqi e-te-qu lik-kil-
me-ši*
**[like a] donkey's feet when crossing the street,
may someone look upon them.**
e-piš-ti ù muš-te-piš-ti
Of the sorceress and 'greater' sorceress,
ina bi-rit kalbêmeš li-su-ru ku-lu-lu-šá
may their crowns fall among dogs,
ina bi-rit ku-lu-lu-šá li-su-ru kalbêmeš
may dogs dance about with their headbands!
e-li-šá qul-mu-ú li-su-ru

And may the axe dance down upon them!
[50] ki-ma piqan sabiti qu-tur-šá li-ib-li
[like a] gazelle having a bowel-movement, may
  their breath be taken away!

BANISHING—USING AN IMAGE OF CHICORY.

[Made of chicory, thyme and granules of grain.]
*at-ti man-nu kassaptušá tetenîpu-šášá 3 arhêmeš
10 u-me mišil u-me*
What is your name sorcer[ess], who has worked
  your spell unceasingly for 3 months plus 10
  and a half days?
ana-ku a-na-áš-šá-kim-ma riqqukukru ta-nat šadî
I raise up the pride of the mountains,
šamhašûtu ti-'-ut ma-a-ti
thyme and the prepared foods of the earth,
*pitiltu pitiltu šá qašdatimeš terinnatu terinnatu šá
še-am ma-la-ti*
acorns and pinecones, that which is full of seed.
*[55] an-nu-ú šá lúkaššapi-ia u kaššapti-ia hi-pa-a
ri-kiš-šu-un*
Yes, my sorcerer and sorceress; I know thee;
  Come, break their knots,
*tir-ra kiš-pu-šá ana me-hi-e amâtimeš-šá ana šá-
a-ri*
turn their spells into storm, their words to
  wind!
li-in-na-áš-pu kiš-pu-šá kîma pû liq-qal-pu kîma

šûmi
May their deceit be blown away as dust, peeled away like layers of garlic [onion],
liš-šá-ah-tu kima suluppi lip-pa-áš-ru kima pitilti
beaten to a pulp like date-fruit and scattered like acorns [seeds]!
ina qí-bit ISTAR DUMU-ZI NA-NA-A be-lit ra-a-mi
By the decree of ISHTAR, TAMMUZ, NANA(Y)A, the Queen of Divine Love,
[60] ù dka-ni-sur-ra be-lit kaššapâtimeš
and of *kanisurra*, the Mistress of Sorceresses!

INCANTATION—CURSING THE EVIL IMAGES.

zêru šá te-pu-šá-ni tu-še-pi-šá-ni ana muh-hi-ku-nu
The hate conjured in your magick, you conjure it against yourself.
zitarrutâa šá te-pu-šá-ni tu-še-pi-šá-ni ana muh-hi-ku-nu; dipalâa-šá te-pu-šá-ni tu-še-pi-šá-nì ana muh-hi-ku-nu kadibbidâa šá te-pu-šá-ni tu-še-pi-šá-ni-ana muh-hi-ku-nu
The murder you have conjured, you have conjured against yourself; the chaos you have conjured, you have conjured against yourself; the disease you have conjured, you have conjured against yourself;
KUS.HUNGA šá te-pu-šá-ni tu-še-pi-šá-ni ana

134

muh-hi-ku-nu dububbâ šá te-pu-šá-ni tu-še-pi-šá-ni ana muh-hi-ku-nu

The *kushunga* you have conjured, you have conjured against yourself; the calamity you have conjured, you have conjured against yourself!

utukku limnu tu-šá-as-bi-ta-in-ni utukku limnu li-is-bat-ku-nu-ši

The evil *utukku* daemon that you allowed to seize me; may the evil *utukku* seize you!

[65] alû limnu tu-šá-as-bi-ta-in-ni alû limnu li-is-bat-ku-nu-ši

The evil *alu* daemon that you allowed to seize me; may the evil *alu* seize you!

etimmu limnu tu-šá-as-bi-ta-in-ni etimmu limnu li-is-bat-ku-nu-ši

The evil spirit that you allowed to seize me; may the evil spirit seize you!

gallû limnu tu-šá-as-bi-ta-in-ni gallû limnu li-is-bat-ku-nu-ši

The evil *gallu* spirit that you allowed to seize me; may the evil *gallu* spirit seize you!

ilu limnu tu-šá-as-bi-ta-in-ni ilu limnu li-is-bat-ku-nu-ši

The evil god that you allowed to seize me; may the evil god seize you!

râbisu limnu tu-šá-as-bi-ta-in-ni râbisu limnu li-is-bat-ku-nu-ši

The evil *rabisu* watcher that you allowed to seize me; may the evil *rabisu* seize you!

[70] lamaštu labasu ahhazu tu-šá-as-bi-ta-in-ni
lamaštu labasu ah hazu-li-is-bat-ku-nu-ši
Lamastu, Labasu, those you allowed to seize me,
  may Lamastu and Labasu seize you!
lúlilû flilitu ardat lili tu-šá-as-bi-ta-in-ni lúlilû
flilitu ardat lili li-is- -bat-ku-nu-ši
Lilu, Lilitu, those nightmares you allowed to
  seize me, may Lilu, Lilitu and those
  nightmares seize you!
ina ni-ši u ma-mit tu-qat-ta-in-ni ina ni-ši u ma-
mit pa-gar-ku-nu liq-ti
You seek to destroy me by covenants and
  magick words, may your life end by covenants
  and magick words.
uz-zi ili šarri BELI u rubî ia-a-ši taš-ku-na-ni
The wrath of God, King and judges you have
  suffered me,
uz-zi ili šarri BELI u rubî a-na ka-a-šu-nu liš-šak-
nak-ku-nu-ši
may the wrath of God, King and judges cause
  you suffering!
[75] a-šu-uš-tu a-ru-ur-tu hu-us qis lìb-bi gi-lit-tú
Pain. Famine. Breaking of the body.
  Uncontrolled trembling;
pi-rit-ti a-dir-ti ia-a-ši taš-ku-na-ni
Fear and depression – all these you have
  planned for me;
a-šu-uš-tu a-ru-ur-tu hu-us qis lìb-bi gi-lit-tú
May pain, famine, body-breaking, uncontrolled
  trembling,

pi-rit-ti a-dir-tu ana ka-a-šú-nu liš-šak-nak-ku-nu-
ši
**fear and depression – and all such be planned
for you!**
aq-mu-ku-nu-ši ina kibrit ellititi u tâbat amurri
**I have burned you with pure sulfur and salt
[from the west];**
[80] al-qut qu-tur-ku-nu ik-kib šamêe
**I have siphoned away your breath to paint the
sky;**
ip-še-te-ku-nu i-tu-ra-ni-ku-nu-ši
Your plans for me have turned against you!

INCANTATION—DEFAMING THE EVIL
IMAGES.
*at-ti man-nu kassaptušá kîma šûti ik-ki-mu ûmi 15
kam*
**Whoever you are, my sorcer[ess], you who blow
like the south-wind on the 15th day,**
ti-il-ti u-me im-ba-ru šá-na-at na-al-ši
**You, whose storm-cloud has gathered for 9
days, whose rain-showers have fallen for a
year,**
urpata iq-su-ra-am-ma iz-zi-za ia-a-ši
You, who has conjured clouds to stand over me:
*[85] a-te-ba-ak-kim-ma ki-ma gal-la-ab šamêe
šâriltânu*
**I rise up to fight you, like the Shredder of the
Heavens, the north-wind!**

ú-sap-pa-ah ur-pa-ta-ki ú-hal-laq ûm-ki
**I scatter your clouds to the wind and destroy
  your storms!**
ú-sap-pa-ah kiš-pi-ki ša tak-ki-mi mu-ša u ur-ra
**I scatter the witchcraft you brought
  unceasingly against me both night and day,**
ù na-áš-pa-rat zitarruti šá tal-tap-pa-ri ia-a-ši
**and the accessories [emissaries] of your evil that
  you unceasingly sent to fight me!**
<unreadable text>

INCANTATION—PROTECTION OF THE
GODS.

[Spoken before image of your god and goddess.]
e-piš-ú-a e-piš-tu-u-a
Evil warlock. Wicked witch.
kaš-šá-pu-u-a kaš-šap-tu-u-a
Evil sorcerer and sorceress.
[120] šá ik-pu-du libbu-ku-nu limuttimtim
You, whose heart has conjured evil,
taš-te-ni-'-a ru-hi-e sab-ru-ti
who have sought out the evil magick,
ina up-šá-še-e la tâbutimeš tu-sab-bi-ta bir-ki-ia
who has bound my legs with evil incantations.
ana-ku ana pu-uš-šur kiš-pi-ia u ru-hi-e-a
**To break my spell and turn your enchantment,
  I have turned**
ina a-mat E-A u ASARI-lú-du GIRRA as-sah-ri
toward the [word] of ENKI and MARDUK

138

[*asariludu*] and GIRRA.

[125] ina mêmeš ša naqbi lìb-ba-ku-nu ú-ni-ih

In water-springs I have brought peace to your heart;

ka-bat-ta-ku-nu ú-bal-li

I have soothed your upset liver;

si-ri-ih lib-bi-ku-nu ú-še-si

I have dispelled your quick-anger;

te-en-ku-nu ú-šá-an-ni

I have confounded your mind;

mi-lik-ku-nu as-pu-uh

I have destroyed your plans;

[130] kiš-pi-ku-nu aq-lu

I have burned your spells;

kip-di lib-bi-ku-nu ú-mat-ti-ku-nu-ši

I have numbered the days of your life.

idiqlat u puratta la te-bi-ra-ni

[The] Tigris and Euphrates [rivers], you will not pass!

iqa u palga la te-it-ti-qa-ni

[The] moat and aqueduct, you will not pass!

dûra u sa-me-ti la tab-ba-lak-ki-ta-ni

[The inner and outer] walls, you will not climb!

[135] abulla u ne-ri-bi-e la tir-ru-ba-ni

[The] gate or entry to the place, you will not pass!

kiš-pi-ku-nu ai ithunimeš-ni

Your spells will not approach me!

a-ma-at-ku-nu ai ik-šu-da-in-ni

Your word cannot reach where I stand!

ina qí-bit E-A SAMAS u MARDUK rubâti dbe-lit ilê

By the decree of ENKI, SAMAS, MARDUK and the Supreme Mistress of the Gods!

INCANTATION—CONSECRATION OF THE DOORWAY.

[Encircle the gateway with blessed pure flour.]

iz-zi-tu-nu šam-ra-tu-nu qas-sa-tu-nu

Fierce, raging, ferocious,

[140] gap-šá-tu-nu nad-ra-tu-nu lim-ni-tu-nu

Overbearing, violent, evil are you!

šá la E-A man-nu ú-na-ah-ku-nu-ši

Who but ENKI can calm you?

šá la ASARI-lú-du man-nu ú-šap-sah-ku-nu-ši

Who but MARDUK [asalluhi] can cool you down?

E-A li-ni-ih-ku-nu-ši

ENKI, may he calm you!

ASARI-lú-du li-šap-ših-ku-nu-ši

MARDUK [asalluhi], may he cool you down!

[145] mêmeš pî-ia mêmeš pi-ku-nu i-šâ-tu

Water is my mouth; fire is your mouth:

pî-ia pî-ku-nu li-bal-li

[May] my mouth extinguish your mouth!

tu-u šá pî-ia tu-u šá pî-ku-nu li-bal-li

[May] the curse of my mouth extinguish the curse of your mouth!

kip-di šá lìb-bi-ia li-bal-la-a kip-di šá lìb-bi-ku-nu

[May] my desired plans extinguish your desired plans!

INCANTATION—AFFIRMATION.

ak-bu-us gallâ-ai- ...

I have taken my enemy down in front of GIRRA!

[150] at-bu-uh gi-ra-ai ahi-

I have killed my enemy by the sacred word!

na mah-ri qu-ra-di GIRRA-

All of this in front of the mighty GIRRA [I have done]!

BANISHING—USING SCATTERED ASHES.

[*Use the scattered ashes of burnt offerings.*]

hu-la zu-ba u i-ta-at-tu-ka

Scatter, flow and drift away from here!

qu-tur-ku-nu li-tel-li šamêe

May your words float away to the sky!

la-'-me-ku-nu li-bal-li dšamšiši

May the sun extinguish the radiance of your ashes!

[155] lip-ru-us ha-ai-ta-ku-nu mâr E-A mašmašu

May your spy be slain, by [MARDUK] the son of ENKI, the Magician!

BANISHING—USING AN IMAGE WITH 9 KNOTS.

[*Tie nine knots into a cord of wool or yarn.*]

šadûu lik-tùm-ku-nu-ši
May the mountain cover you!

šadûu lik-la-ku-nu-ši
May the mountain hold you back!

šadûu li-ni-ih-ku-nu-ši
May the mountain calm you down!

šadûu li-ih-si-ku-nu-ši
May the mountain overpower you!

[160] šadûu li-te-'-ku-nu-ši
May the mountain swallow you up!

šadûu li-ni-'-ku-nu-ši
May the mountain pass reject you!

šadûu li-nir-ku-nu-ši
May the mountain cliff kill you!

šadûu li-qat-tin-ku-nu-ši
May the mountain wastelands make you thin!

šadûu dan-nu elî-ku-nu lim-qut
May the [mighty] mountain avalanche fall upon you!

[165] ina zumri-ia lu-u tap-par-ra-sa-ma
Indeed, you shall be shaken from my body!

BANISHING RITE—BURNING THE IMAGES.

i-sa-a i-sa-a ri-e-qa ri-e-qa
Go away! Go away! Be gone! Be gone!

bi-e-šá bi-e-šá hi-il-qa hi-il-qa
Stay away! Stay away! Flee! Flee!
dup-pi-ra at-la-ka i-sa-a u ri-e-qa
Get off! Go away! Stay away! Be gone!
limuttu-ku-nu ki-ma qut-ri li-tel-li šamêe
**Your evil spell, like smoke, may it rise ever
  skyward into nothing!**
[170] ina zumri-ia i-sa-a
From my body, keep off!
ina zumri-ia ri-e-qa
From my body, be gone!
ina zumri-ia bi-e-šá
From my body, depart!
ina zumri-ia hi-il-qa
From my body, flee!
ina zumri-ia dup-pi-ra
From my body, get off!
[175] ina zumri-ia at-la-ka
From my body, go away!
ina zumri-ia la tatârâ
From my body, turn away!
na zumri-ia la tetehêe
My body, do not approach!
ina zumri-ia la taqarubâ
My body, do not come near!
ina zumri-ia la tasaniqâqa
My body, do not touch!
[180] ni-iš SAMAS kabti lu ta-ma-tu-nu
**By the breath of SAMAS, Radiant One, you are
  commanded!**

ni-iš E-A BEL naqbi lu ta-ma-tu-nu
By the breath of ENKI, Lord of the Deep, you are commanded!
ni-iš ASARI-lú-du maš-maš ilimeš lu ta-ma-tu-nu
By the breath of MARDUK [*asalluhi*], Magician of the Gods, you are commanded!
ni-iš GIRRA qa-mi-ku-nu lu ta-ma-tu-nu
By the breath of GIRRA, your Executioner, you are commanded!
ina zumri-ia lu-u tap-par-ra-sa-ma
Indeed you shall be kept from my body!

THE MAQLU SERIES – TABLET VI

INCANTATION—RITE OF PROTECTION.
EN-LIL qaqqadi-ia pa-nu-ú-a u-mu
ENLIL is my head, the face that meets the day,
duraš ilu git-ma-lu la-mas-sat pa-ni-ia
URAS, the 'perfect god' is my protecting face,
kišadi-ia ul-lu šá NIN-LIL
My neck – the necklace of NINLIL,
idâmeš-ai dgam-lum šá NANNA-SIN amurri
My arms – the crescent swords of NANNA-SIN,
[5] ubânâtumeš-ú-a isbînu esemtu IGIGI
My fingers become the *tamarisk* [of ANU], my bones become the IGIGI;
la ú-šá-as-na-qa ru-hi-e a-na zu-um-ri-ia
They do not allow sorcery to penetrate my body.

LUGAL-edin-na dla-ta-raq irti-ia
Lugaledinna and **Latark** are my chest,
kin-sa-ai dmu-úh-ra šêpâll-ai šá ittanallakaka
My knees – *Muhra*, my feet which carry me
ka-li-ši-na lu lah-mu
are each *Lahmu*.
[10] at-ta man-nu ilu lim-nu šá lúkaššapi u kaššapti
What is your name, Evil God, you whom my
**   sorcerer and sorceress**
iš-pu-ru-niš-šú a-na dâki-ia
have conjured to kill me?
lu-ú e-ri-ta la tal-la-ka
When you arise, do not move!
lu-ú sal-la-ta-ta la te-tib-ba-a
When you are asleep, do not awaken!
amâtemeš-ka lu ishašhuru ina pân ili u šarri li-nu-šú
[May] your words become a bitter apple for
**   God and King!**
[15] ul-te-sib ina bâbi-ia LUGAL-gir-ra ilu d-an-nu
I set at my door, Mighty GIRRA [*lugal-girra*],
**   avenger of ANU**
sukkal ilimeš PAP-SUKKAL
and the messenger of gods, NABU [*papsukkal*]
**   also.**
li-du-ku lúkaššapi u kaššapti
They may kill my sorcerer and sorceress;
li-tir-ru amât-sa a-na pî-šá

They may turn their words back in their
  mouth!

BANISHING—USING A CHICORY-PLANT IMAGE.

riqqukukru-ma riqqukukru
Chicory, chicory!
riqqukukru ina šadânimeš ellûtimeš qud-du-šu-ti
Chicory from the brilliant divine mountains!
sihrûtimeš tir-hi šá e-ni-ti
Small *tirhu*-vessel of the priestess,
sihrâtimeš terinnâtimeš šá qa-aš-da-a-ti
Small pinecones of *hierodule* [*qasdati*],
[30] al-ka-nim-ma šá lúkaššapi-ia u kaššapti-ia
come: of my sorcerer and sorceress
dan-nu hipameš rikis-sa
break their charged knots!
tir-ra kiš-pi-ša a-na me-hi-e amâtemeš-šá ana šâri
**Turn their magick wild on them, [turn their]
  words into wind!**
li-in-ni-eš-pu kiš-pi-ša ki-ma pû
**May their sorcery be blown away on them like
  granules!**
li-ša-as-li-mu-ši ki-ma di-iq-me-en-ni
May [their sorceries] make them black like ash!
[35] ki-ma libitti igâri liš-hu-hu kiš-pu-šá
May their spells break apart over the wall!
šá kaššapti-ia lip-pa-tir rikis lib-bi-šá
May the heart of my sorceress be melted away!

BANISHING—USING A CHICORY-PLANT IMAGE.

riqqukukru-ma riqqukukru
Chicory, chicory!
riqqukukru ina šadânimeš ellûtimeš qud-du-šu-ti
Chicory from the brilliant divine mountains!
sihrûtimeš tir-hi šá e-ni-ti
Small *tirhu*-vessel of the priestess,
[40] sihrâtimeš terinnâtimeš šá qa-aš-da-a-ti
Small pinecones of *hierodule* [*qasdati*],
al-ka-nim-ma šá lúkaššapi-ia u kaššapti-ia
come: of my sorcerer and sorceress
dan-nu hipâa rikis-sa
break their charged knots;
ù mimma ma-la te-pu-šá nu-tir a-na šâri
and everything you have bewitched, we turn into wind!

BANISHING—USING A CHICORY-PLANT IMAGE.

e kaššapti-ia e-li-ni-ti-ia
My sorceress, my nightmare!
[45] -a-bu la taš-ku-ni tu-qu-un-tu
You have not given up your confounding!
am-me-ni ina bîti-ki i-qat-tur qut-ru
Why does smoke still rise from your house?
a-šap-pa-rak-kim-ma -ti
I am sending you my evil spell!
ú-sap-pah kiš-pi-ki ú-tar amâtemeš-ki ana pî-ki
I destroy your deceit! I destroy your mouth!

BANISHING—USING A CHICORY-PLANT IMAGE.

la-am NIN-gir-su ina šadî il-su-u da-la-la

In front of NINGIRSU, in the mountains, a divine song of victory was raised,

[50] la-am kal i-lu-u ana na-kas isbîni

in front of everyone, it raised up and cut tamarisk.

kassaptušá ana annanna apil annanna tu-kap-pa-ti abnêmeš

Damn the sorceress who gathers stone [images] against __ son of __,

taš-te-ni-'-e li-mut-ta

and prepare evil sorcery,

a-za-qa-kim-ma kima iltani amurri

I blow on you like the cold north-wind and piercing west-wind!

ú-sap-pah urpata-ki ú-hal-laq u-um-ki

I destroy the clouds of your enchantment and clear away your bad weather,

[55] ù mimma ma-la te-pu-ši ú-tar a-na šâri

and I turn everything you have bewitched into wind!

BANISHING—USING A CHICORY-PLANT IMAGE.

at-ta e šá te-pu-ši ka-la-a-ma

You who conjures all types of magick,

[70] min-mu-u te-pu-ši ia-a-ši u šim-ti-ia

what you have bewitched, me and my [image],
riqqukukru šá šadîi ihtepi rikis-ki
chicory from the mountain will break your knots!
šá imitti-ki u šumêli-ki šâru lit-bal
May the wind blow away what is left [and right] of you!

CONSECRATION—USING A SULFUR IMAGE.

kibri-dit ellitu mârat šamêe rabûtimeš ana-ku
I am pure sulfur, I am born of the Daughter of the Heavens,
A-NIM ib-na-ni-ma E-A EN-LIL ú-še-ri-du-ni-
ANU created me, ENKI and ENLIL brought me down to this planet...
<unreadable text>

BANISHING—USING A SULFUR IMAGE.

[85] kibri-dit ellitu šam-KUR.KUR šam-mu qud-du-šu ana-ku
Pure sulfur, *kurkur*-weed – I am the pure weed.
e-pi-šu-u-a apqallu šá apsî
My sorcerer is wise in the ways of the Deep
e-pi-iš-tu-u-a mârat da-nim šá šamêe
My sorceress is born of the daughter of the Sky-God ANU.
ki-i e-te-ni-ip-pu-šu-ni ul i-li-'-a-in-ni

**Although they have bewitched me, they have
not overwhelmed me.**

ki-i e-pu-šu-si-na-a-ti iš-te-'u-si-na-a-ti

**Since they have conjured sorcery and evil
magick,**

[90] e-til-la-a kima nûnêmeš ina mêmeš-ia

Make them rise like a fish in my pond,

kîma šahi ina ru-šum-ti-ia

Like a pig in my sty,

kîma šam-maštakal ina ú-sal-li

Like a *matakal*-weed in my fields,

kîma šamsassati ina a-hi a-tap-pi

Like the reed-grass on the riverbank,

kîma zêr isuši ina a-hi tam-tim

Like a seed of the black tree on shoreline,

[95] e-šá dillat-e e-šá dillat-e

**[in all these] where my divine support exists,
where my divine support exists,**

nar-qa-ni a-na qaq-qa-ri

May you be emptied out onto the ground,

šá tu-na-sis-a-ni kim-mat-ku-nu ia-a-ši

You, who have shook your head at me!

BANISHING—USING A SULFUR IMAGE.

dit qaqqadi-ia kibri-dit pa-da-at-ti

The god is my head, the sulfur is my [image]

šêpâ-ai na-a-ru šá man-ma la idûu ki-rib-šá

**My feet are the river in whose depths no one
knows.**

150

[100] šam-AN.HUL.LA pû-ia tâmtu ta-ma-ta
rapaštumtum rit-ti
The *anhulla*-plant is my mouth, the sea of
  distant TIAMAT is my hand...

INCANTATION—CONSECRATION OF
THE SALT.

at-ti tabtu šá ina áš-ri elli ib-ba-nu-ú
You are the salt that was formed in a the 'Pure
  Place'.
ana ma-ka-li-e ilimeš rabûtimeš i-šim-ki EN-LIL
A meal for the Great Gods, you have been fated
  by ENLIL;
ina ba-li-ki ul iš-šak-kan nap-tan ina é-kur
without you there is no meal in the E.KUR,
ina ba-li-ki ilu šarru BELU u rubû ul is-si-nu qut-
rin-nu
without you, God, King and Master cannot
  smell the incense.
[115] ana-ku annanna apil annanna šá kiš-pi su-
ub-bu-tu-in-ni
I, __ , son of __ have beheld the sorcery,
up-šá-še-e li-'-bu-in-ni
allowed the baneful plot to fester:
putri kiš-pi-ia tabtu pu-uš-ši-ri ru-hi-e-a
break the spells, salt! Dissolve the sorceries!
up-ša-še-e muh-ri-in-ni-ma kîma ili ba-ni-ia
Remove the baneful plan from me! Like unto
  my creator,

lul-tam-mar-ki
I will be free to give adoration!

INCANTATION—RITE OF PROTECTION.

[120] e kaššapti-ia lu rah-ha-ti-ia
[I laugh at you] my sorceress, medicine-man;
šá a-na bêriám ip-pu-hu išâta
who has lit the fires for one side,
a-na bêri iš-tap-pa-ra mâr šip-ri-ša
but sends her [watcher] to both sides,
ana-ku i-di-ma at-ta-kil ta-ka-lu
I know, I have strong conviction;
ina -ia ma-sar-tú ina bâbi-ia az-za-qap ki-din-nu
**I have set a watcher in my house; at my gate, a
protector,**
[125] ismaiâli-ia al-ta-me subâtú-li-in-na
**I have enchanted a scarf to wrap around my
bed,**
ina rêš ismaiâli-ia a-za-raq šamnuhurtu
**I have sprinkled *asadoetida* at the head of my
bed,**
dan-na-at šamnuhurtu-ma ú-na-ha-ra kal kiš-pi-ki
**so the strong *asafoetida* fragrance will end all of
your sorceries!**

INCANTATION—RITE OF PROTECTION.

e kaššapti-ia e-li-ni-ti-ia
My sorceress, [evil informant], I laugh at you,

šá tattallaki kal mâtâti
you, who blows back and forth over the lands,
ta-at-ta-nab-lak-ka-ti kal šadânimeš-ni
**you, who crosses back and forth over the
mountains,**
ana-ku i-di-ma at-ta-kil ta-ka-lu
I know – and I have a firm conviction,
[140] ina- -ia ma-sar-tú ina bâbi-ia az-za-qap ki-din-nu
**in my house I have stationed a watcher, at the
gate I put a protector;**
ina imitti bâbi-ia u šumêli bâbi-ia
at the right of my gate and left of my gate
ul-te-iz-ziz LUGAL-gir-ra u MIS-lam-ta-è-a
I have set *lugal-girra* and *meslamtaea*;
*ilimeš šá ma-sar-te na-si-ih lib-bi muš-te-mi-du
kalâtimeš*
**may these "guardian gods" burst the insides of
the one who 'steals reason'!**
kassaptuli-du-ku-ma ana-ku lu-ub-lut
May they kill the sorceress that I may live!

THE MAQLU SERIES – TABLET VII

INCANTATION—RITE OF PROTECTION.
rit-ti dman-za-ád GIR.TAB-meš
My hand is *manzad*, my scorpion;
ši-i kassaptuú-nak-ka-ma kiš-pi-šá
[she], the sorceress, gathers her spells,

ú- -pah-kim-ma ki-ma marrati ina šamêe
I [cover] you like the rainbow in the sky,
ú-za-qa-kim-ma kîma iltâni amurrî
I blow on you like the north-wind, the west-
   wind,
[5] ú-sa-ap-pah urpata-ki ú-hal-laq ûm-ki
I destroy your clouds and dispel your bad
   weather!
ú-sap-pah kiš-pi-ki šá tak-ki-mi mu-šá u ur-ra
I destroy the sorcery you have gathered up both
   day and night,
ù na-áš-pa-rat zitarrutâa šá tal-tap-pa-ri ia-a-ši
and all malefic messages you send my way.
sa-lil nêbiru sa-lil ka-a-ru
NEBIRU [*boat of heaven's crossing*] calls, the
   harbor calls,
mârêmeš malâhi ka-li-šú-nu sal-lu
the sailors are resting all the while;
[10] elî isdalti ù issikkuri na-du-u hur-gul-lu
the door and bolt are wrapped up,
na-da-at ši-pat-su-un šá dsiris u NIN-giš-zi-da
the incantations are laid down of SIDURI and
   NINGISHZIDA,
šá lúkaššapi-ia u kaššapti-ia ip-šá bar-tum amât
limuttimtim
the sorcery, the incantations, the evil speech,
   the evil word of my sorcerer and sorceress,
ai ithunimeš.ni ai i-ba-'-u-ni
should not come near; will not come in!
bâba ai êrubûnimeš.ni ana bîti

The door [gate] is barred; [they should not]
enter the house!
[15] NIN-giš-zi-da li-is-suh-šú-nu-ti
NINGISHZIDA, throw them out!
lib-bal-ki-tu-ma e-pi-šá-ti-šu-nu li-ba-ru
[May] they kneel down to catch their helpers!
ilu šarru BELU ù rubû lik-kil-mu-šú-nuina
**[May] God, King and Master look at their evil
unfavorably.**
ina qâtê ili šarri BELI u rubî ai ú'si kaš-šap-ti
**In [the] power of my God and king, the
sorceress will not escape!**
a-na-ku ina qí-bit MARDUK BEL nu-bat-ti
**(But) I act in alignment with MARDUK, the
Master of Magicians,**
[20] ù ASARI-lú-du BEL a-ši-pu-ti
**MARDUK [asariludu], Master of the
Incantations,**
min-mu-ú e-pu-šu lu ku-ši-ru
may everything I have done here be successful!
ip-še te-pu-šá-ni li-sa-bil šâra
**[May] the sorceries you have conjured against
me turn into wind!**

INCANTATION—CONSECRATING THE
WATERS.
a-ra-hi-ka ra-ma-ni a-ra-hi-ka pag-ri
I sanctify you, my self; I sanctify you, the whole

of my body;

ki-ma dsumuqân ir-hu-ú bu-ul-šú

like the *sumuqan* sanctifies his cattle,

[25] sênu im-mir-šá sabîtu ar-ma-šá atânu mu-ur-šá

the ewe with her lamb, the gazelle with her kid,
   the she-donkey with her foal,

isepinnu irsitimtim ir-hu-ú irsitimtim im-hu-ru zêr-šá

[like] the plow sanctifies the earth, and the
   earth receives [from the] plow, its seeds,

ad-di šipta a-na ra-ma-ni-ia

I have conjured an incantation upon myself!

li-ir-hi ra-ma-ni-ma li-še-se lum-nu

May it sanctify me and drive evil away!

ù kiš-pi ša zumri-ia li-is-su-hu

May they tear away the sorcery from my body,

[30] ili-meš rabûti-meš

the Great Gods!

INCANTATION—CONSECRATING THE OILS.

šamnu ellu šamnu ib-bu šamnu nam-ru

Pure oil, clean [light] oil, shinning oil!

šamnu mu-lil zumri šá ilimeš

Oil [pure] which cleanses the gods!

šamnu mu-pa-áš-ši-ih širšir-a-na šá a-me-lu-ti

Oil which soothes the muscles of humans!

šaman šipti šá E-A šaman šipti šá ASARI-lú-du

Oil consecrated to the incantation of ENKI,
  oil of the incantation of MARDUK
  [*asariludu*]!

[35] ú-ta-hi-id-ka šaman tap-šu-uh-ti
I have let you drip with the oil that cleanses
šá E-A id-di-nu a-na pa-áš-ha-a-ti
that ENKI has given forth to heal [with].
ap-šu-uš-ka šaman balâti
I have rubbed you with the 'Oil of Life'
ad-di-ka šipat E-A BEL eri-du NIN-igi-kug
have placed you next to the incantation of
  ENKI, Lord of ERIDU and NINIGIKUG
at-ru-ud a-sak-ku ah-ha-zu
have chased away the *asakku* [the seizer],
[40] šu-ru-up-pu-u ša zumri-ka
[the] chill is [removed] from your body.
ú-šat-bi qu-lu ku-ru ni-is-sa-tú šá pag-ri-ka
[I have] removed the frightful sound, the fear,
  the trembling of your body,
ú-pa-áš-ši-ih šir-a-ni mi-na-ti-ka la tâbâtimeš
[have] healed the tendons of your ailing
  members.
ina qí-bit E-A šar apsî
Upon ENKI, Lord of the Deep,
ina tê ša E-A ina šipat ASARI-lú-du
with the formula of ENKI, [along] with the
  incantation of MARDUK [*asariludu*],
[45] ina ri-kis ra-ba-bu šá GU-LA
[Clothed] in the 'large garments' of GULA,
ina qâtê pa-áš-ha-a-ti šá NIN-DIN-UG-GA

with the healing hands of NINDINUGGA,
ú NIN-a-ha-qud-du BEL šipti
and of NINAHAQUDDU, Master of
  Incantation,
ana annanna apil annanna šub-šu-ma E-A šip-
at-ka šá balâti
let __, son of __ know, ENKI and you
  'Incantation of Life'!
7 apqallê šu-ut eri-du li-pa-áš-ši-hu zumur-šu
[May the] seven *apqallu* of Eridu heal his body!

INCANTATION—PREPARING IMAGES
FOR BURNING.

[50] EN-LIL qaqqadi-ia MULKAK.SI.ŠÁ la-a-ni
ENLIL is my head, the star *kaksisa* is my form;
pûtu SAMAS nap-hu
**[the] forehead is SAMAS [*usually 'light of cres-*
cent'],**
idâ-ai isgamlu šá bâb MARDUK
[my] arms [are] the curved sword of the Gate
  of MARDUK,
uzna-a-a li-'-u šêpâII-a-a lah-mu mu-kab-bi-sa-at
lah-me
[my] ears are a (divine) tablet, my stomping feet
  [are a] snake.
at-tu-nu ilimeš rabûtimeš šá ina šamêe nap-ha-tu-
nu
You, Great Gods, who are lit in the heavens,
[55] kîma an-na ku an- ip-šu bar-tum amât lemut-

tim

Like the evil sorceries, spells and malediction

la itehhûmeš-ku-nu-ši la i-sa-ni-qú-ku-nu-ši

do not come near you, or even push up close,

ip-šu bar-tú amât lemut-tim la itehhû-ni la isan-niqû-ni ia-ši

so may the baneful sorceries, spells and malediction not come near to me, or even push up close against me!

MAQLU INCANTATION—BURNING THE IMAGES.

at-ti man-nu kassaptušá êpušušu sal-mi

Who are you, sorceress? You who has an [image] of me,

it-tu-lu la-a-ni êpušušu la-mas-si

who has observed my form and fashioned an [image],

[60] i-mu-ru bal-ti ú-šar-ri-hu ga-ti

has seen my strength, has fashioned my [image],

ú-sab-bu-u nab-ni-tú

has studied the shape of my form,

ú-maš-ši-lu bu-un-na-ni-e-a

has reproduced [carefully] my features,

ub-bi-ru mi-na-ti-ia

has bound my appendages [members],

ú-kas-su-u meš-ri-ti-ia

has bound up my appendages [members],

[65] ú-kan-ni-nu ma-na-ni-e-a
has distorted my nervous system;
ia-a-ši E-A maš-maš ilimeš ú-ma-'-ra-an-ni
**[but] ENKI, Enchanter of the Gods, has sent
me;**
ma-har SAMAS sa-lam-ki e-sir
in front of SAMAS I have drawn your [image].
la-an-ki ab-ni bal-ta-ki a-mur
**I have drawn your [image]. I have observed
your strength,**
gat-ta-ki ú-šar-ri-ih nab-nit-ki ú-sab-bi
**I have made your [image] and caught the shape
of your form,**
*[70] i-na dnisaba ellitimtim bu-un-na-an-ni-ki ú-
maš-šil*
I have duplicated your [image] using pure flour,
mi-na-ti-ki ub-bi-ir meš-ri-ti-ki ú-kas-si
**I have bound your appendages; I have bound
up your appendages,**
ma-na-ni-ki ú-kan-ni-in
I have distorted your nervous system;
ip-šú te-pu-šin-ni e-pu-uš-ki
**I have conjured on you the spell that you did
cast on me.**
mi-hir tu-šam-hir-in-ni ú-šam-hir-ki
**I have let you have your evil encounter that you
suffered me!**
[75] gi-mil tag-mil-in-ni ú-tir ag-mil-ki
**I have let you have your revenge that you
suffered me!**

kiš-pi-ki ru-hi-ki ru-si-ki ip-še-te-ki lim-ni-e-te
**Your sorcery, your spells, your evil, your
malignance,**
up-šá-še-ki ai-bu-te
your evil plans,
na-áš-pa-ra-ti-ki šá li-mut-ti
your evil messages,
râm-ki zêr-ki dipalû-ki zitarrutû-ki
[your] love, hate, imbalance and murder,
[80] kadibbidû-ki dubbubu-ki li-kil-lu rêš-ki
**[your] disease and calamities; may your head
stop thinking!**
*it-ti mêmeš šá zumri-ia u mu-sa-a-ti šá qâtê-ia liš-
šá-hi-it-ma*
**With [pure] water of my body, purifying water
of my hands, may your evil be removed**
*a-na muh-hi-ki u la-ni-ki lil-lik-ma ana-ku lu-ub-
lut*
and from your head and form, that I may live!
e-ni-ta li-na-an-ni ma-hir-ta lim-hur-an-ni
**May divine grace bless me and good fortune
come to me!**

BANISHING—USING AN IMAGE WITH
7 KNOTS.

[Tie seven knots into a cord of wool or yarn.]
ba-'-ir-tú šá ba-'ra-a-ti
Catcher of catchers!
[85] kassaptušá kaššapâtimeš

Sorceress of sorceresses!
šá ina sûqâtameš-ta na-da-tu še-is-sa
Who, in the streets, has spread their net,
ina ri-bit âli it-ta-na-al-la-ka ênâ-šá
whose eyes, dart about in the city square;
lúetlêmeš âli ub-ta-na-'
she targets the men in the city,
it-ti lúetlêmeš âli ub-ta-na-'-in-ni ia-a-ši
with the men of the city, she has targeted me
   [too].
[90] ardâtimeš âli is-sa-na-hur
the girls of the city, she cavorts with,
it-ti ardâtimeš âli is-sa-na-hur-an-ni ia-a-ši
with the girls of the city, she cavorts with me
[too].
e ú-ba-'-kim-ma lúkurgarêmeš lúeš-še-bi-e
I seek ... against you, *kur-garras* and *essebi*
rikis-ki a-hi-pi
I will break your bindings!
lúkaššapêmeš li-pu-su-ki rikis-ki a-hi-pi
May warlocks bewitch you, but I will break
   your bindings!
[95] kaššapâtimeš li-pu-ša-ki rikis-ki a-hi-pi
May witches bewitch you, but I will break your
   bindings!
lúkurgarêmeš li-pu-šu-ki rikis-ki a-hi-pi
***Kurgarras* bewitch you, but I will break your**
   bindings!
lúeš-še-bu-ú li-pu-šu-ki rikis-ki a-hi-pi
***Essebu* bewitch you, but I will break your**

bindings!

nar-šin-du-umeš li-pu-šu-ki rikis-ki a-hi-pi

Narsindus bewitch you, but I will break your bindings!

mušlahhêmeš li-pu-šu-ki rikis-ki a-hi-pi

Snake-charmers bewitch you, but I will break your bindings!

[100] a-gu-gil-lumeš li-pu-šu-ki rikis-ki a-hi-pi

Agulgillu bewitch you, but I will break your bindings!

a-mah-has li-it-ki a-šal-la-pa lišân-ki

I devour your face. I rip out your tongue,

ú-ma-al-la ru-'-a-ta ênáII-ki

I fill your eyes with my spit,

ú-ša-lak a-hi-ki lil-lu-ta

I make your arms loose their strength [*"to become weak"***].**

ú ak-ka-a-ši ru-uq-bu-ta ú-ša-lak-ki

and for you to eat, I leave out rotten refuse,

[105] ù mimma ma-la te-te-ip-pu-ši ú-tar ana muh-hi-ki

and everything you have conjured against me, I turn back onto your head!

BANISHING—USING AN IMAGE WITH 3 KNOTS.

[*Tie three knots into a cord of wool or yarn.*]

ep-ši-ki ep-še-ti-ki ep-še-et ep-ši-ki

Your enchantment and magick, the sorcery of

your sorceress,

ep-še-et mu-up-pi-še-ti-ki

[the] sorcery of your sorcerer,

E-A maš-maš ilimeš ú-pat-tir-ma mêmeš uš-ta-bil

ENKI, Father of Magicians, has undone [it all]
and turned [it] to water!

pî-ki lim-nu e-pi-ra lim-la

May your evil mouth be filled with dirt from
the earth!

[110] lišân-ki šá limuttimtim ina qî-e lik-ka-sir

May your evil tongue be tied up with a string!

ina qî-bit den-bi-lu-lu BEL balâti

[All this] by the decree of *Enbilulu*, Master of
Life!

BANISHING RITE—BURNING THE
CORD-KNOT IMAGES.

ki-is-ri-ki ku-us-su-ru-ti

Your bound knots,

ip-še-ti-ki lim-ni-eti up-šá-še-ki ai-bu-ti

your evil spells and evil manifestations,

na-áš-pa-ra-tu-ki šá limuttimtim

your evil intentions spoken,

*[115] ASARI-lú-du maš-maš ilimeš ú-pat-tir-ma ú-
šá-bil sara*

MARDUK [*asariludu*], Master of Magicians,
has done and removed [all of this]!

pî-ki lim-nu epirahi.a lim-ma-li

May your evil mouth be filled up with dirt from

the earth,

lišan-ki šá limuttimtim ina qí-e lik-ka-sir

and may your evil tongue be tied up with a
string!

ina qí-bit den-bi-lu-lu BEL balâti

[All this] by the decree of *Enbilulu*, Master of
Life!

INCANTATION—PURIFICATION RITE.

[*The hands and body are washed then anointed.*]

am-si qa-ti-ia ub-bi-ba zu-um-ri

I have washed my hands; I have purified my
body

[120] *ina mêmeš naqbi ellûtimeš šá ina eri-du ib-
ba-nu-u*

in [pure] waters which come from Eridu
proper;

mimma lim-nu mimma lâ tâbu

may all diseased spirits, all of the evil spirits
and misfortune

šá ina zumri-ia šêrêmeš-ia šir'ânêmeš-ia bašûu

that in my body, my form and my being exists,

*lumun šunâtimeš idâtimeš ittâtimeš limnêtimeš lâ
tâbâtimeš*

anxiety by way of evil and unfavorable dreams,
harbingers of doom,

*lumun šîrîmeš ha-tu-ti par-du-ti lemnû-timeš lâ
tâbûtimeš*

anxiety by way of false dreams, evil visions and

misfortune,

[125] *lipit qâti hi-niq šu'i ni-iq ni-qi nêpeš-ti barû-ti*

by laying-of-hands, strangulation of life, of divination,

šá at-ta-ta-lu u-me-šam

by all of that which I see every day,

ú-kab-bi-su ina sûqi e-tam-ma-ru ina a-ha-a-ti

and that which I step upon in the street and what I see around me,

še-ed lem-utti ú-tuk-ku lim-nu

the evil *sedu*, the evil *utukku*,

mursu di-'di-lip-ta

illness, headache, upset,

[130] *qu-lu ku-ru ni-is-sa-tú ni-ziq-tú im-tu-uta-ni-hu*

terror, fear, quivering, worry, depression, apathy,

'ú-a a-a hu-su-su qis lib-bi

pains, aches, cramps, leprosy,

gi-lit-tum pi-rit-tum a-dir-tum

more fear, obsession, terror,

ár-rat ilimeš mi-hir-ti ilimeš ta-zi-im-ti

sin, the unfavorably hand and wrath of Gods,

ni-iš ilî ni-iš ilî ni-iš qâti ma-mit

curses born of oaths to God and the oath-swearing raised hand,

[135] *lum-nu kiš-pi ru-hi-e ru-si-e up-šá-še-e lem-nu-ti šá amêlûtimeš*

sorcery, spells, evil manifestations of humans,

it-ti mêmeš šá zumri-ia u mu-sa-a-ti šá qâte-ia
**may they all, with the clean water of my body
and hands,**
liš-šá-hi-it-ma ana muhhi salam nig-sagilêe lil-lik
**be sent to the deceiver whose [image] is before
me!**
salam nigsagilêe ár-ni di-na-ni li-iz-bil
May my sin carry my [image] instead of me!
su-ú-qu ù su-lu-ú li-pat-ti-ru ár-ni-ia
**May the causeway and path cleanse me of
the sin!**
[140] e-ni-tum li-na-ni ma-hir-tum lim-hur-an-ni
**May the grace [of the highest] bless me, may
favorable conditions come to me!**
am-hur mi-ih-ru lim-hu-ru-in-ni
**I have lived through [this] experience [enough];
may it now turn favorably toward me!**
*u-mu šul-ma arhu hi-du-ti šattu hagalla-šá li-bil-
la*
**May the day bring health, the month bring joy
and the year its prosperity.**
EA, SAMAS u MARDUK ia-a-ši ru-sa-nim-ma
ENKI, SAMAS and MARDUK come to my aid!
lip-pa-áš-ru kiš-pu ru-hu-u ru-su-u
**May the evil sorcery, the evil spells, all be
dissolved [to nothingness]!**
[145] up-šá-šu-ú lim-nu-ti šá a-me-lu-ti
May the evil manifestations of men and the
ù ma-mit lit-ta-si šá zumri-ia
baneful oath sword all now leave my body!

MAQLU INCANTATION—RITE FOR JUST BEFORE DAWN.

te-bi še-e-ru mesâa qâte-ia
Dawn is coming forth, my hands are washed;
-ma qaq-qa-ru mu-hur up-ni-ia
[my iniquity] is cleansed, my sin is absolved.
šá kassaptuú-kaš-šip-an-ni
Because the sorceress has enchanted me,
[150] eš-še-bu ú-sa-li-'-an-ni
the wicked witch has made me sick,
SAMAS pi-šir-ta li-bil-am-ma
SAMAS, I call on you to bring me salvation!
irsitimtim lim-hur-an-ni
May the earth protect me!

MAQLU INCANTATION—RITE AT DAWN.

it-tam-ra še-e-ru pu-ut-ta-a dalati
Dawn has come forth; the doors have opened;
a-lik ur-hi it-ta-si abulla
the traveler has passed through [the gate];
[155] mâr šipri is-sa-bat har-ra-na
the messenger has taken to the road.
e-piš-tum e te-pu-šin-ni
Witch, hey, did you try to bewitch me?
ra-hi-tum e tu-ri-hi-in-ni
Enchantress, hey, did you try to enchant me?
ú-tal-lil ina na-pa-ah dšamši
[Well], now I am freed with the radiant light of the rising sun;

mimma ma-la te-pu-ši ù tu-uš-te-pu-ši
Whatever witchcraft you believe you have done,
[160] li-tir-ru-ma li-is-ba-tu-ki ka-a-ši
may it all turn back upon you – yes, you!

MAQLU INCANTATION—RITE FOR JUST AFTER DAWN.

še-ru-um-ma še-e-ru
Morning, [glorious] morning!
an-nu-ú šá lúkaššapi-ia u kaššapti-ia
[Honestly] my sorcerer and sorceress
*it-bu-nim-ma kîma mârêmeš lúnâri ú-lap-pa-tú
nu-'-šú-nu*
have plucked at their cords like minstrels.
ina bâbi-ia iz-za-zi PALIL
At my gate stands PALIL,
[165] ina rêš ismaiâli-ia iz-za-zi LUGAL-edin-na
at the head of my bed guards *Lugal-edinna,*
a-šap-pa-rak-kim-ma šá bâbi-ia PALIL
I send you from my gate, PALIL;
šá rêš ismaiâli-ia LUGAL-edin-na
and from my bed, *Lugal-edinna.*
mîli bêri dib-bi-ki mîli har-ra-ni a-ma-ti-ki
Your speech will turn around on you [like a]
   flood on the streets,
ú-tar-ru kiš-pi-ki ru-hi-ki ú-sa-ab-ba-tu-ki ka-a-ši
your sorceries, charms and spells will [come
   back] to seize you, yes you!

MAQLU INCANTATION—MORNING RITE.

[170] ina še-rì misâa qâtâ-ai

In dawn-time, my hands have been cleansed,

šur-ru-ú dam-qu li-šar-ra-an-ni

may a prosperous beginning start for me;

tu-ub lìb-bi tûbub šêri li-ir-te-da-an-ni

**may happiness and good fortune ever follow
  alongside me,**

*e-ma ú-sa-am-ma-ru su-um-mi-ra-ti-ia lu-uk-šu-
ud*

**whatever it is that I desire, may I obtain my
  desires,**

šunât e-mu-ru ana damiqtimtim liš-šak-na

whenever I dream, may those be favorable,

*[175] ai ithâa ai isniq mimma lim-nu mimma lâ
tâbu*

**and [keep away] anything evil, anything
  malevolent,**

ru-hi-e šá lúkaššapi u kaššapti

**any evil enchantment of the sorcerer and
  sorceress,**

*ina qí-bit EA, SAMAS u MARDUK u ru-bâti belit
i-li*

**by the decree of ENKI, SAMAS, MARDUK
  and the Queen, Lady of the Gods [of the
  heavens]!**

THE MAQLU SERIES – TABLET VIII

INCANTATION—CLOSING RITES.

un-du kassaptui-bir nâra
After the sorceress has crossed the river,
- -u iš-la-a -
she escaped me by going under the Deep.
[35] e-piš-ti áš-bat ina ni-bi-ri
My sorceress sits lonely in NI.BI.RI
- -šu-uš ka-a-ri
[My sorceress sits lonely] on the shore.
ub-ta-na-'-an-ni ia-ši ana sa-ha-li-ia
She still seeks me, seeks her revenge.
li- -ši-ma apqallêmeš šá apsî
May the *apqalle* of the Deep go to her,
- -zi ni-me-qí ni-kil-ti E-A iq-bu-u la-pan-šá
**[let her taste] the clever wisdom of ENKI, King
  of the Deep!**
[40] E-A šar apsî lih-da-a pa-ni-šá
May you rejoice with ENKI, King of the Deep!
li-sa-hi-ip-ši be-en-na te-šá-a ra-i-ba
May [my] paralysis and anger be subsided,
li-tir hur-ba-as-sa
[my] fear be removed,
- -pu-luh-ta šá i-da-a eli-šá
[I have held] fear against you,
ana elî salmânimeš-šá misâa qâtâ-ia
[but now] I wash my hands over their [images],
[45] i-na riqqukukri šá šadî riqquburâši elli
with *chicory*, pine and cypress;

i-na šam-DIL.BAT mu-ul-lil amêli misâa qâtâ-ia
with the *dilbat*-weed that cleanses humans, I
have washed my hands.
e-te-lil ana-ku -ina elî sêri-šá
pure I have become [like the water] more than
she can,
kiš-pu-šá lim-lu-u-sêru
Her sorceries, in the desert [may they rot].
amâtemeš-šá šâru-lit-bal
I carry away her words [to the wind]
[50] ù mimma ma-la e-pu-šu li-tur ana šâri
and every enchantment she has manifested, I
throw to the wind!

INCANTATION—CLOSING RITES.
ultu SUMU-qân ina šadî ilsûû da-la-la
After *Sumuqan* had begun the victory song on
the mountain;
ultu kal i-lu-ú a-na na-kas isbîni
(and) after everyone had ascended to cut
***tamarisk*;**
áš-bat-ma ummu - -šú
the mother and father sat down.
áš-bu-ma i-ma-li-ku- ahu -
they convene to counsel the bother and sister.
[55] at-ti man-nu kassaptušá ia-a-ši u ram-ni-ia
Whoever you are, sorceress, who I have now
bewitched,
e-piš-tú e-pu-šá kiš-pi ik-ši-pu

Witch who has bewitched [and who I have now
  bewitched],
kiš-pu-šá lu-u šâru kiš-pu-šá lu-u me-hu-ú
may your spells be wind, may your spells be lost
  in a storm,
kiš-pu-šá lu-u pu-u lit-tap-ra-šá-du elî-šá
may your spells be grains of dust that fly up in
  your face!
<unreadable text>
...[and may] eagles and vultures scour your
  dead body!
qu-lu hur-ba-šu lim-qu-ut elî-ki
Pain and fear, may it befall you!
kalbu u kalbatu li-ba-as-si-ru-ki
Hound and bitch, may they tear you apart!
kalbu u kalbatu li-ba-as-si-ru šêrêmeš-ki
Hound and bitch, may they tear your flesh
  away!
ina qí-bit EA, SAMAS u MARDUK u rubâti MAH
By decree of ENKI, SAMAS, MARDUK and
  the Queen (goddess) MAH!

INCANTATION—CLOSING RITES.
[90] at-ta silli at-ta ba-aš-ti
You are my strength [like] a shield;
at-ta dšêdi at-ta ga-at-ti
You are the 'guardian god' of my form,
at-ta pa-da-at-ti at-ta du-u-ti
You are my [image], my barrier [wall],

<unreadable text>
e tam-hur kiš-pi e tam-hur ú-pi-ši

**Hey, spell-crafter! Hey, evil-doer! You are
finished!**

*[95] KI.MINA šag-gaš-tú KI.MINA na-kas napiš-
timtim*

**The same for a murderess, the same for the
remover of life,**

KI.MINA ru-'-ut-ta -ab-tu

the same for friendship-breakers,

KI.MINA kadibbidâ KI.MINA dipa-lâa

**the same for the seizing disease, the same for
the worldly injustice,**

KI.MINA zêru KI.MINA ši- -pi-ši

the same for hate, the same for [violence],

limnûtimeš - -ti

[the same for all of the] evils of the [world].

[100] at-ta ia-ú a-na-ku ku-ú

Great God, you are mine and I am yours,

man-ma-an ai il-mad-ka mimma lim-nu ai ithi-ka

**may none but me counsel with you, may evil
never come close to you,**

ina qí-bit EA, SAMAS MARDUK

by the decree of ENKI, SAMAS, MARDUK

u rubâti MAH

and the Queen (goddess), MAH!

[*End of Ceremonial Tablet Series*]

THE

MAQLU

APPENDIX

MAQLU SERIES – TABLET IX
(FRAGMENTS)

<unreadable text>

[**Paraphrase:** "when you perform the rites of the *Maqlu* tablet series" follow the following methods: When using the incantations that describe an object, have a representation of that object; when defacing the material images, follow a like-is-like preference: so a figure of salt can be crushed, of dough can be 'eaten' or 'devoured', an image made of wax should be held over a fire until the wax drips – all following in correlation with the series-texts.]

Materials to fashion the images

ÉN NUSKU šur-bu-u ma-lik ilîmeš rabûtimeš salam lipî
**"Glorious NUSKU, Counselor of the Gods..." –
an image of *talcum*.**
ÉN GIRRA BELu git-ma-lu gaš-ra-a-ta na-bi šum-ka salam siparri kibri-dit
**"GIRRA, lord and master, perfect and
powerful..." – an image of *copper* or *sulfur*.**
[30] ÉN GIRRA a-ri-ru bu-kur da-nim salam si-parri
"GIRRA, born of ANU..." – an image of *copper*.

ÉN GIRRA a-ri-ru mar a-nim salam lîši
**"GIRRA, raging fire born of ANU..." – an
  image of *dough*.**
ÉN GIRRA gaš-ru u-mu na-an-du-ru salam titi
**"GIRRA, bringer of terrible storms..." – an
  image of *clay*.**
ÉN GIRRA šar-hu bu-kur da-nim salam itti
**"GIRRA, powerful son of ANU..." – an image
  of *asphalt*.**
ÉN ki-eš libeš ki-di-eš salam kuspi
"kes libes kides..." – an image of *sesame-butter*.
*[35] ÉN e-pu-šú-ni etenippušûnimeš.ni salam itti
šá gassa bullulu*
**"They have bewitched me, they have hexed..."
  – an image of *asphalt* covered with *plaster*.**
ÉN at-ti man-nu kassaptušá ina nâri im-lu-' tîta-ai
**"Whoever you are, sorceress, who gathers
  clay..."**
salam titi šá lipâ bullulu
**– an image of *clay* covered with *talcum* [salt,
  powder].**
ÉN at-ti man-nu kassaptušá tub-ta-na-in-ni
**"Whoever you are, sorceress, who visits me
  unceasingly..."**
salam isbîni salam iserini
– an image *tamarisk*-wood and/or one of *cedar*.
*[40] ÉN kaššaptum mut-tal-lik-tum šá sûqâ-timeš
salam tîti*
**"Sorceress who wanders the streets..." – an
  image of *clay*.**

lipû ina rêš lib-bi-sa êra ina kalâtimeš-šá tu-sa-na-áš

(You put the *talcum* on the stomach [of the image] and stuff her kidneys with wood.)

ÉN ta ši-na mârâtimeš da-nim šá šamêe salam lipî hi-im-ma-ti

"Two are the daughters of the Sky-God ANU..." – an image of *talcum* and *garbage*.

ÉN kassaptunir-ta-ni-tum salam dakî

"Sorceress, murderess..." – an image of *wax*.

ÉN dit ellu nam-ru qud-du-šú ana-ku salam itti

"I am the light, pure and shinning..." – an image of *asphalt*.

[45] ÉN la-man-ni su-tu-ú e-la-mu-ú ri-da-ni

"The man from the SUTI-tribe sees me, the ELAMITE chases me..."

salam itti šá kibri-dit

– an image of *asphalt* next to one of *sulfur*.

ÉN at-ti man-nu kassaptušá iq-bu-u a-mat limut-timtim-ia ina libbi-šá

"Who are you, evil sorceress, in whose heart the evil spell against me resides..."

salam titi ina kunukki arqi amâta-šá ta-šá-tar

– an image of *clay* (you should write the 'word' on a green cylinder-seal).

ÉN at-ti ia-e šá te-pu-šin-ni ISTAR - -

"You, who has betwitched my goddess..."

[50] ha-ha-a šá ú-tu-ni um-me-en-na šá di-qa-ra

– an image using clumps of *ash* from the furnace, and *soot* clinging to the pots.

ina mêmeš ta-mah-ha-ah-ma ana qaqqad salam titi ta-tab-bak

(You mix it with water and pour it over the head of your *clay* image.)

ÉN šá e-pi-šá-an-ni ul-te-piš-an-ni maqur titi

"She was has bewitched me..." – use the [image] in a ship or *boat of clay*

2 salmu ina libbi

with two figures inside.

ÉN maqurri-ia NANNA-SIN ú-še-piš

"My boat, NANNA-SIN possesses..." – an image.

[55] - -salam lîši ÉN

... of *dough*.

<unreadable text>

ÉN rit-tu-um-ma rit-tum rit-ta lipî

"Hand! Hand..." – an image of a *hand*, made of *talcum*.

ÉN rit-tum-ma rit-tum <unreadable text>

[60] ÉN biš-li biš-li bal-lu-ur-ta qanêmeš šá gi-sal-li

"Boil! Boil..." – an image and a *cross* made of *pipes of reed*.

2 qanâtimeš šá ma-lu-ú ina muh-hi a-ha-meš ta-par-rik

(Two pipes are filled with blood and excrement, lay them in a 'cross' pattern

ina ni-ri ina qabal -

in the middle of [*presumably "your magick circle"*].)

2 salam lipi 2 salam -
Two figures of *talcum* and two figures of ...
ina ap-pa-a-ta šá bal-lu-ur-ta te-en-ni-ma
place these at the four points of the cross.)
<unreadable text>
ÉN at-ta man-nu kassaptušá zitarrutâa êpušuš
"Whoever you are, sorceress, who has committed murder..."
hu-sab- -
– an image using three branches...
ÉN nir-ti-ia kaššapti-ia u ku-šá-pa-ti-ia
"My murderess, my sorceress and the 'greater' sorceress..."
lipû uban titi- -
– an image of *talcum*...
[70] ÉN šá dšamšiši man-nu abu-šú
"Who is the father of the sun-god..."
markas šipâti pisâti riksê ta-rak-kas
– an image with a white piece of *wool* tied in three *knots*.
ÉN i-pu-šá-ni i-te-ni-ip-pu-šá-ni
"I am being bewitched..."
markas šipâti pisâti riksê ta-rak-kas
– an image with a white piece of *wool* tied in seven *knots*.
<unreadable text>
[80] ÉN at-ti man-nu kassaptušá te-te-ni-ip-pu-šá
"Whoever you are, sorceress, you who unceasingly enchants..."
riqqukukru šamhašûtu ù pû ta-šar-rap

– burn the image with *chicory*, *thyme* and
  granules *of grain*.

<unreadable text>

*[95] arki-su ÉN UDUG HUL EDIN.NA.ZU.ŠE a-
di ni-pi-ši-ša*

...thereafter, recite the incantation: "Evil
  demon, to your desert..." to the outer
  threshold;

tamannu-ma mashata bâbâtime te-sir

[then] encircle the entrance-ways with blessed
  [pure] flour.

*a-na bîti terrub-ma a-šar ma-aq-la-a taq-lu-u a-
meš ŠUB.ŠUB.DI*

Return to the house – place where you have
  performed the MAQLU – libate with water.

*ÉN a-nam-di šipta a-na pu-uh-ri ilîmeš ka-la-a-
ma tam-annunu*

"I cast an incantation upon the assembly of All
  the Gods."

ÉN EN-LIL qaqqadi-ia pa-nu-ú-a u-mu- -

"ENLIL is my head, I rise to face the day..."

*[100] ÉN e-piš-ta qu-um-qu-um-ma-ta riqqukuk-
ru*

"The sorceress is a *qumqummatu*..." – an image
  with *chicory*.

<unreadable text>

"Hey, my sorceress, my nightmare..." – use
  chicory.

*ÉN la-am NIN-gir-su ina šadî il-su-ú da-la-a
riqqukukru*

"In front of NINGIRSU..." – use *chicory*.
[105] ÉN e kassaptuú-kaš-šip-an-ni riqqukukru
"The sorceress has bewitched..." – use *chicory*
lipû lu-ba-ri-e parsûtimeš
also *talcum* and cut pieces of *clothing*.
<unreadable text>
[110] ÉN kibri-dít kibri-dít - -dít kibri-dít
"Sulfur. Sulfur..." – use *sulfur*.
<unreadable text>

[Paraphrase: Working through the list of incantations found throughout the *Maqlu*, the ritual tablet describes the presence of an herb a stone or an image such as it already appears within the text of the incantation.**]**

<unreadable text>

[Paraphrase: Numerous lines appear here that match with the openings of various incantations in the later part of the MAQLU series. All of them denote *"handwashing"* as the ritual action, or else the sprinkling of blessed waters.**]**

[End of the MAQLU series.]

THE ORIGINAL HARDCOVER 2-VOLUME SET

SUMERIAN RELIGION

*Introducing the Anunnaki Gods
of Mesopotamian Neopaganism*

Mardukite Liber-50

by Joshua Free

BABYLONIAN MYTH & MAGIC

*Spiritual Traditions and Mysticism
in Mesopotamian Anunnaki Religion*

Mardukite Liber-51+E

by Joshua Free

SYSTEMOLOGY
The Pathway to Self-Honesty

GO FURTHER AND BE

CRYSTAL CLEAR

CRYSTAL CLEAR

(Handbook for Seekers)

Mardukite Systemology Liber-2B
by Joshua Free

Take control of your destiny
and chart the first steps
toward your own spiritual evolution.
Realize new potentials of the
Human Condition with
a Self-guiding handbook for
Self-Processing toward
Self-Actualization
in Self-Honesty using actual
techniques and training
provided for the coveted
"Mardukite Systemology Grade-III
Self-Defragmentation Course Program"
—once only available
directly and privately from
the underground Systemology Society.

Discover the amazing power behind the
applied spiritual technology
used for counseling and advisement in
the tradition of Mardukite Zuism.

SYSTEMOLOGY

The Pathway to Self-Honesty

THE WAY INTO THE
FUTURE

A Handbook for
the New Human

a collection of writings by
Joshua Free
as selected by James Thomas

now available as a
Collector's Edition Hardcover

Here are the basic answers to what has held
Humanity back from achieving its ultimate
goals and unlocking true power of the Spirit
and the highest state of Knowing and Being.

"*The Way Into The Future*" illuminates the
Pathway leading to Planet Earth's true
"metahuman" destiny. With *excerpts from*
"*Tablets of Destiny*," "*Crystal Clear*,"
"*Systemology—Original Thesis*" and
"*The Power of Zu.*" You can help shine clear
light on anyone's pathway!

Carefully selected by Mardukite
Publications Officer, James Thomas,
this critical *collection of eighteen*
articles, lecture transcripts and reference
chapters by Joshua Free is sure to be
not only a treasured part
of your personal library,
but also the perfect
introduction for all friends,
family and loved ones.

(*Basic Grade-III Introductory Pocket Anthology*)

19 95   20 20

JOSHUA FREE

PUBLISHED BY THE **JOSHUA FREE** IMPRINT REPRESENTING

The Founding Church of Mardukite Zuism

THE JOSHUA FREE IMPRINT
JFI PUBLICATIONS

MARDUKITE
ZUISM

mardukite.com

www.ingramcontent.com/pod-product-compliance
Lightning Source LLC
Chambersburg PA
CBHW011237120626
46549CB00009B/3305